Vincent van Gogh

GREAT ACHIEVERS:

LIVES OF THE PHYSICALLY CHALLENGED

ARTIST

Peter Tyson

Chelsea House Publishers

New York • Philadelphia

On the Cover: *Self-Portrait Before Easel* (1888) by Vincent van Gogh. Oil on canvas. Van Gogh Museum, Amsterdam, The Netherlands.

CHELSEA HOUSE PUBLISHERS

EDITORIAL DIRECTOR   Richard Rennert
EXECUTIVE MANAGING EDITOR   Karyn Gullen Browne
COPY CHIEF   Robin James
PICTURE EDITOR   Adrian G. Allen
CREATIVE DIRECTOR   Robert Mitchell
ART DIRECTOR   Joan Ferrigno
PRODUCTION MANAGER   Sallye Scott

GREAT ACHIEVERS: LIVES OF THE PHYSICALLY CHALLENGED

SENIOR EDITOR   Kathy Kuhtz Campbell
SERIES DESIGN   Basia Niemczyc

Staff for **VINCENT VAN GOGH**
EDITORIAL ASSISTANT   Scott D. Briggs
PICTURE RESEARCHER   Pat Burns

First Printing

1   3   5   7   9   8   6   4   2

Library of Congress Cataloging-in-Publication Data

Tyson, Peter.
Vincent van Gogh: artist / Peter Tyson.
p. cm.—(Great achievers)
Includes bibliographical references and index.
Summary: Briefly examines the life of the renowned Dutch painter and traces the development of his art.
ISBN 0-7910-2422-9
      0-7910-2423-7 (pbk.)
1. Gogh, Vincent van, 1853–1890—Juvenile literature. 2. Painters—Netherlands—Biography—Juvenile literature. [1. Gogh, Vincent van, 1853–1890. 2. Artists.] I. Title. II. Series: Great achievers (Chelsea House Publishers)
ND653.G7T95 1996   95-17496
759.9492—dc20   CIP
[B]   AC

FRONTISPIECE:

Vincent van Gogh painted Self-Portrait with a Gray Hat *while he was living with his brother Theo in Paris, France, in early 1887. During his 23-month stay in Paris, van Gogh produced 22 of the 35 self-portraits that exist today.*

CONTENTS

GREAT ACHIEVERS

LIVES OF THE PHYSICALLY CHALLENGED

JIM ABBOTT
baseball star

LUDWIG VAN BEETHOVEN
composer

LOUIS BRAILLE
inventor

CHRIS BURKE
actor

ROY CAMPANELLA
baseball star

RAY CHARLES
musician

BOB DOLE
politician

STEPHEN HAWKING
physicist

ERNEST HEMINGWAY
writer

JACKIE JOYNER-KERSEE
champion athlete

HELEN KELLER
humanitarian

RON KOVIC
antiwar activist

MARIO LEMIEUX
ice hockey star

MARLEE MATLIN
actress

MARY TYLER MOORE
actress

FLANNERY O'CONNOR
author

ITZHAK PERLMAN
violinist

FRANKLIN D. ROOSEVELT
U.S. president

HENRI DE TOULOUSE-LAUTREC
artist

VINCENT VAN GOGH
artist

STEVIE WONDER
musician

A Message for Everyone

Jerry Lewis

Close to half a century ago—when I was the ripe old age of 23—an incredible stroke of fate rocketed me to overnight stardom as an entertainer. After the initial shock wore off, I began to have a very strong feeling that, in return for all life had given me, I must find a way of giving something back. At just that moment, a deeply moving experience in my personal life persuaded me to take up the leadership of a fledgling battle to defeat a then little-known group of diseases called muscular dystrophy, as well as other related neuromuscular diseases—all of which are disabling and, in the worst cases, cut life short.

In 1950, when the Muscular Dystrophy Association (MDA)—of which I am national chairman—was established, physical disability was looked on as a matter of shame. Franklin Roosevelt, who guided America through World War II from a wheelchair, and Harold Russell, the World War II hero who lost both hands in battle, then became an Academy Award–winning movie star and chairman of the President's Committee on Employment of the Handicapped, were the exceptions. One of the reasons that muscular dystrophy and related diseases were so little known was that people who had been disabled by them were hidden at home, away from the pity and discomfort with which they were generally regarded by society. As I got to know and began working with people who have disabilities, I quickly learned what a tragic mistake this perception was. And my determination to correct this terrible problem soon became as great as my commitment to see disabling neuromuscular diseases wiped from the face of the earth.

I have long wondered why it never occurs to us, as we experience the knee-jerk inclination to feel sorry for people who are physically disabled, that lives such as those led by President Roosevelt, Harold Russell, and all of the extraordinary people profiled in this Great Achievers series demonstrate unmistakably how wrong we are. Physical disability need not be something that blights life and destroys opportunity for personal fulfillment and accomplishment. On the contrary, as people such as Ray Charles, Stephen Hawking, and Ron Kovic prove, physical disability can be a spur to greatness rather than a condemnation of emptiness.

In fact, if my experience with physically disabled people can be taken as a guide, as far as accomplishment is concerned, they have a slight edge on the rest of us. The unusual challenges they face require finding greater-than-average sources of energy and determination to achieve much of what able-bodied people take for granted. Often, this ultimately translates into a lifetime of superior performance in whatever endeavor people with disabilities choose to pursue.

If you have watched my Labor Day Telethon over the years, you know exactly what I am talking about. Annually, we introduce to tens of millions of Americans people whose accomplishments would distinguish them regardless of their physical conditions—top-ranking executives, physicians, scientists, lawyers, musicians, and artists. The message I hope the audience receives is not that these extraordinary individuals have achieved what they have by overcoming a dreadful disadvantage that the rest of us are lucky not to have to endure. Rather, I hope our viewers reflect on the fact that these outstanding people have been ennobled and strengthened by the tremendous challenges they have faced.

In 1992, MDA, which has grown over the past four decades into one of the world's leading voluntary health agencies, established a personal achievement awards program to demonstrate to the nation that the distinctive qualities of people with disabilities are by no means confined to the famous. What could have been more appropriate or timely in that year of the implementation of the 1990 Americans with Disabilities Act than to take an action that could perhaps finally achieve the alteration of public perception of disability, which MDA had struggled over four decades to achieve?

On Labor Day, 1992, it was my privilege to introduce to America MDA's inaugural national personal achievement award winner, Steve Mikita, assistant attorney general of the state of Utah. Steve graduated magna cum laude from Duke University as its first wheelchair student in history and was subsequently named the outstanding young lawyer of the year by the Utah Bar Association. After he spoke on the Telethon with an eloquence that caused phones to light up from coast to coast, people asked me where he had been all this time and why they had not known of him before, so deeply impressed were they by him. I answered that he and thousands like him have been here all along. We just have not adequately *noticed* them.

It is my fervent hope that we can eliminate indifference once and for all and make it possible for all of our fellow citizens with disabilities to gain their rightfully high place in our society.

ON FACING CHALLENGES

John Callahan

I was paralyzed for life in 1972, at the age of 21. A friend and I were driving in a Volkswagen on a hot July night, when he smashed the car at full speed into a utility pole. He suffered only minor injuries. But my spinal cord was severed during the crash, leaving me without any feeling from my diaphragm downward. The only muscles I could move were some in my upper body and arms, and I could also extend my fingers. After spending a lot of time in physical therapy, it became possible for me to grasp a pen.

I've always loved to draw. When I was a kid, I made pictures of everything from Daffy Duck (one of my lifelong role models) to caricatures of my teachers and friends. I've always been a people watcher, it seems; and I've always looked at the world in a sort of skewed way. Everything I see just happens to translate immediately into humor. And so, humor has become my way of coping. As the years have gone by, I have developed a tremendous drive to express my humor by drawing cartoons.

The key to cartooning is to put a different spin on the expected, the normal. And that's one reason why many of my cartoons deal with the disabled: amputees, quadriplegics, paraplegics, the blind. The public is not used to seeing them in cartoons.

But there's another reason why my subjects are often disabled men and women. I'm sick and tired of people who presume to speak for the disabled. Call me a cripple, call me a gimp, call me paralyzed for life.

Just don't call me something I'm not. I'm not "differently abled," and my cartoons show that disabled people should not be treated any differently than anyone else.

All of the men, women, and children who are profiled in the Great Achievers series share this in common: their various handicaps have not prevented them from accomplishing great things. Their life stories are worth knowing about because they have found the strength and courage to develop their talents and to follow their dreams as fully as they can.

Whether able-bodied or disabled, a person must strive to overcome obstacles. There's nothing greater than to see a person who faces challenges and conquers them, regardless of his or her limitations.

Vincent van Gogh probably painted this hardy-looking self-portrait in September 1889—nearly a year after he cut off part of his left ear—to reassure his mother that he was feeling well. Although it is the last self-portrait he painted, van Gogh depicted an unsettling image of himself as a young-looking, clean-shaven peasant.

1

A PERFECT VOLCANO

IN OCTOBER 1888, Vincent van Gogh received the letter he had been awaiting for months: It was from artist Paul Gauguin, writing to say he was coming to Arles, a village in Provence, the region of southern France where van Gogh then lived. Ever since he had moved to Arles eight months earlier, van Gogh had been trying to convince his friend Gauguin to join him there to paint as head of an "artists colony" van Gogh was forming.

Van Gogh was at the apex of his artistic career. Though he was just 35 years old and had only been painting for six years, he had achieved a unique style that ultimately would make him one of the most popular of modern painters, and his work is reproduced more often than that of any other artist. During that fall, he had painted some of his greatest masterpieces, including *Bedroom at Arles* and *The Night Café,* and to decorate the room in his tiny apartment where Gauguin would stay, he

Van Gogh's second version of Bedroom at Arles, *in which the self-portrait he sent to his mother appears, was painted from memory while he recuperated at the asylum in Saint-Rémy in 1889. Van Gogh told his brother Theo in a letter the year before that he wanted the original painting of his room "to express an absolute restfulness"; he wished to hang it in his bedroom for decoration before Paul Gauguin's arrival in Arles in October 1888.*

painted several canvases of sunflowers that today remain some of his most characteristic and beloved oils.

Yet even as his brush brought him to the highest levels of artistic achievement, his health, both mental and physical, had fallen to a dangerously weak state. Throughout his life, from his student days through his years as an art dealer, then a preacher, and finally a painter, van Gogh had neglected his physical welfare. Often he did not have enough money to feed himself properly, but increasingly he willfully neglected his body because the life of the mind—whether it was preaching the gospel in London's ghettos or painting in the farm fields of Arles—always took precedence over that of the body. Van Gogh's workaholism, which he pushed to a demented degree,

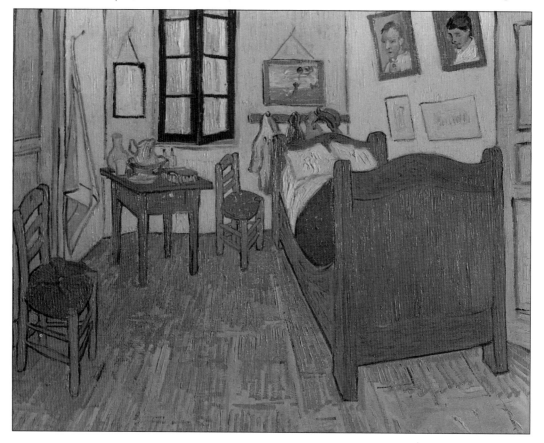

eventually took a toll on his mental well-being. As a loner driven to unceasing toil and continual self-chastisement, he had always appeared strange to others, but by the time Gauguin arrived at his doorstep in October 1888, van Gogh was on the verge of having a nervous breakdown.

But van Gogh saw himself as simply caught up in the swirl of excitement and revival then sweeping through the artistic world. Several new artistic movements, centered in Paris, had begun to shake the rafters of the centuries-old structure of classic academic painting. Ever since the Baroque and Rococo periods during the 17th and 18th centuries, painting had relied on romantic and allegorical themes, ennobled landscapes, and a rigid, precise style taught in the great art academies. Van Gogh's countrymen alone contributed enormously to the prodigious artistic accomplishments during the 17th century: Jacob van Ruisdael (1628–1682) perfected deep perspective in his landscape paintings; Peter Paul Rubens (1577–1640) and Jan Vermeer (1632–1675) exploited color to previously unknown degrees; and Rembrandt Harmensz van Rijn (1606–1669) mastered the self-effacing self-portrait.

At its best, traditional Neoclassical painting, in which artists of the mid–18th century tried to re-create the art of ancient Greece and Rome, had achieved sublime heights. By the early 19th century, however, some painters began to break away from strict Neoclassicism. For example, as chief painter to Emperor Napoléon I, the French artist Jacques-Louis David executed standard academic paintings, such as *The Distribution of the Eagles* (1810). But in earlier works, such as *The Death of Socrates* (1787) and *Brutus and the Bringing Home of the Bodies of His Sons* (1789), he broke from tradition by eschewing sentimentality and excessive expressions of emotion and aimed to express his thoughts on virtue and his political views during the French Revolution. These works can be seen as the beginnings of "modern art." By the middle of the century, in the face of transformations brought about by the Industrial Revolution, including polluted cities and a more striking separation of rich and poor, many budding painters sought to break wholly free from the academic style.

For some, that break came with Impressionism. This new movement rejected the standard religious scenes and stilted portraits espoused by the academies in favor of painting nature and people in their everyday surroundings. Instead of the photograph-like accuracy found in the older style of painting, Impressionists painted with a deliberate, sketchlike imprecision, dabbing brightly colored oil paint in swift strokes onto the canvas in an attempt to catch the changing light on a wheat field or on the facade of a cathedral. While the academics painted in indoor studios, the Impressionists headed out-of-doors with newly available tin tubes of oils to paint directly from nature, often working all day in a field or on a busy Parisian thoroughfare.

Several other movements that evolved in the mid-to-late 19th century complemented Impressionism. Painters like Jean-Baptiste Camille Corot and Jean-François Millet set the stage for Impressionism by painting from nature and choosing subjects, like peasants in the fields during harvesttime, that were far humbler than the grand themes, such as the crowning of Napoléon I, taken on by academic painters. Georges Seurat and his disciple Paul Signac created scenes using dots of paint rather than brushstrokes in a quasi-Impressionist style known as Pointillism. Finally, a group of painters known as Postimpressionists emerged. Like Impressionists, they painted natural and pastoral subjects with bright colors and a freehanded style, but they put the style in a broader context by choosing a wider scope of subjects, ranging from intimate portraits of women dressing to portraits of Tahitian natives. Among the leading Postimpressionists of the day were Paul Cézanne, Edgar Degas, Paul Gauguin, and Vincent van Gogh.

Even as he painted the greatest masterpieces of his career, however, van Gogh considered himself a secondary artist, an apprentice ever struggling to find his style and perfect his craft after a late start. Though many today consider him to have been a genius, van Gogh himself refused to acknowledge his own talent. To van Gogh, Gauguin, who seemed much older than van Gogh but was actually only five years his senior, represented the true modern artist, a man of great stature in the artistic world, whose level van Gogh, Gauguin's adoring apprentice, aspired to attain. Earlier that year, he wrote in a letter to Gauguin, "I always think my artistic conceptions extremely ordinary when compared to yours." When Gauguin announced he was coming to Arles, van Gogh, as a gift, painted a symbolic portrait of himself as a *bonze,* a Japanese monk, awaiting his master. In a letter to Gauguin—van Gogh was a prodigious correspondent—he described the painting's bold use of colors, which had now become his trademark. "The ashen-gray color that is the result of mixing malachite green with an orange hue, on pale malachite ground, all in harmony with the reddish-brown clothes. But as I also exaggerate my personality, I have in the first place aimed at the character of a simple bonze worshipping the Eternal Buddha."

To van Gogh, Gauguin's imminent arrival in Arles not only vindicated his talent but fulfilled another long-held dream of his: to form an artists' commune in the south of France. Such a colony would be far away from the competitive and constraining atmosphere of Paris, at that time the heart of the art world. "My dear comrade Bernard," he wrote to his friend the painter Émile Bernard, "more and more it seems to me that the pictures which must be made, so that painting should be wholly itself, and should be raised to a height equivalent to the serene summits which the Greek sculptors, the German musicians, the writers of French novels reached, are beyond the powers of an isolated individual; so they will probably be created by groups of men combining to execute an idea held in common." Van Gogh imagined a beneficial sharing of the talents of different artists. "One may have a superb orchestration of colors but lack ideas," he continued in the letter to Bernard. "Another is cram-full of new concepts, tragically sad or charming, but does not know how to express them." Was he thinking of himself (as colorist) and Gauguin (as thinker)? In any case, Gauguin's coming meant his long-cherished commune was underway at last, so van Gogh awaited his friend's arrival in late October with great anticipation.

But trouble began almost as soon as Gauguin arrived. "Between two such beings as he and I, the one a perfect volcano, the other boiling inwardly too, a sort of struggle was preparing," Gauguin later wrote. It was a struggle that, within just two months, would play itself out tragically, with Gauguin leaving Arles for good and van Gogh launched on a downward spiral of intermittent madness mixed with intense creativity that would lead, a year and a half later, to his untimely death at age 37.

The scene was set for friction. Gauguin disliked Arles from the beginning, calling it "the filthiest place in the Midi," as the surrounding region along the Mediterranean is known. To Gauguin, the town, peasants, and landscape—where the sun shone more brightly than it did in Paris and that had inspired van Gogh to his most exalted creativity—seemed "small, paltry." And in van Gogh's cramped, four-room apartment, which van Gogh lovingly referred to as the Yellow House, Gauguin found "a disorder that shocked me." The untidiness, in Gauguin's eyes, ran to all aspects of van Gogh's life. To put things in a semblance of order, the older man bought furniture, put the pair's scant funds into a box with a sheet to note any withdrawals, and took on the role of cook. "Once,"

During the summer and fall of 1888, van Gogh worked on his series of Sunflowers, *many of which he had planned to use to decorate Gauguin's room in the Yellow House. The series of paintings, today his most popular, are depicted in bright colors, especially his favorite, yellow. He built up the pigment of the flowers' petals and centers so much that they actually project from the plane like relief sculpture.*

Gauguin recalled later, "Vincent wanted to make a soup. How he mixed it I don't know; as he mixed his colors in his pictures, I dare say. At any rate, we couldn't eat it."

Under such shaky circumstances, the two set to work. They painted together, often side by side, in a vineyard, in an Arles public garden, and in the Alyscamps, an avenue of tombs left over from Roman times. To his brother Theo, with whom he corresponded throughout his life, van Gogh wrote that Gauguin was "a very great artist and a very excellent friend." In the evenings, often until the early hours of the morning, the two debated aspects of art theory in the Arlesian cafés and in the Yellow House. Gauguin tried in vain to teach van Gogh to paint abstractions from memory, but van Gogh had always painted what he saw before him, whether it be a wheat field or a line of boats along the shore. To van Gogh, abstraction was, as he explained to his brother, "an enchanted territory, old man, and one quickly finds oneself up against a wall." The roommates also argued about portraiture, says van Gogh, "until our nerves were so strained there wasn't a spark of vital warmth left in us."

Indeed, their relationship was highly charged. Earlier he had confessed to Theo that his arguments with Gauguin "are terribly electric, sometimes we come out of them with our heads as exhausted as a used electric battery." Of a portrait Gauguin made of him painting a still life of flowers, van Gogh later asked his brother, "Have you seen the portrait that he did of me painting some sunflowers? Afterward my face got much more animated, but it was really me, very tired and charged with electricity as I was then." In the portrait, van Gogh clearly looks exhausted. For his part, Gauguin reported in his 1903 memoir *Avant et après* (Before and after), that, upon seeing the finished portrait, van Gogh remarked, "It is certainly I, but it's I gone mad."

Such intensity could only put a great strain on their relationship. By early December, only six weeks after his arrival, Gauguin began dropping hints of leaving Arles. "My situation here is very awkward," he wrote to his friend Emile Schuffenecker. "I owe a great deal to [Theo] van Gogh [who had recently purchased 300 francs worth of Gauguin's pottery and agreed to pay him a monthly allowance on the condition that Gauguin send one painting per month to him, thereby enabling Gauguin to stay in Arles] and to Vincent and, in spite of some discord, I cannot be angry with an excellent fellow who is sick, who suffers, and who asks for me. . . . In any event I shall stay here, but my departure will always be a possibility." Soon thereafter Gauguin announced to Theo that he must leave because of "incompatibility of temper."

Van Gogh, in his keyed-up state, naturally took his friend's news hard. "Ever since the question arose of my leaving Arles he had been so queer that I hardly breathed any more," Gauguin later admitted to a friend. "He even said to me: 'You are going to leave,' and when I said 'Yes,' he tore a sentence from a newspaper and put it into my hand: '*The murderer has fled.*'" Gauguin recalled that by mid-December van Gogh had become alternately "rough and noisy, and then silent." One night, Gauguin claimed he caught his friend sneaking over to his bedside in the middle of the night. When he asked "What's the matter with you, Vincent?" van Gogh turned and, without a word, got back into his bed and dropped instantly into a heavy sleep.

On the night of December 23, 1888, van Gogh finally snapped. "I had bolted my dinner, I felt I must go out alone and take the air along some paths that were bordered by flowering laurel," Gauguin wrote in *Avant et après*. (Written 15 years after the fact, Gauguin's memoir has proven inaccurate and self-serving in places, but it is the only testimony of the tragic events of that night.) "I had almost crossed Place Victor Hugo when I heard behind me a well-known step, short, quick, irregular. I turned about on the instant as Vincent rushed toward me, an open razor in his hand. My look at that moment must have had great power in it, for he stopped and, lowering his head, set off running towards home." Gauguin slept that night in a hotel. The next morning he returned to the Yellow House, where he found a commotion outside. People were milling about and whispering. A policeman approached him.

"What have you done to your comrade, Monsieur?" Gauguin recalled the policeman asking him.

"I don't know. . . ."

"Oh, yes . . . you know very well. He is dead."

The two went upstairs. Gauguin remembered, "It took me a long time to get my wits together and control the beating of my heart." They went into van Gogh's tiny bedroom. "In the bed lay Vincent, rolled up in the sheets, all in a ball; he seemed lifeless," Gauguin recollected. "Gently, very gently, I touched the body, the heat of which showed that it was still alive. For me it was as if I had suddenly got back all my energy, all my spirit. Then in a low voice I said to the police superintendent: 'Be kind enough, Monsieur, to awaken this man with great care, and if he asks for me, tell him that I have left for Paris. The sight of me might prove fatal to him.'"

Van Gogh was taken to the Hôtel-Dieu, the main hospital in Arles, and put under the care of Dr. Félix Rey.

It seems that after the incident with the razor the night before, van Gogh had gone back to the Yellow House, where he sliced off part of his left ear with the razor. Several days later, an Arlesian newspaper reported that "Last Sunday night at half past eleven a painter named Vincent Vaugogh [sic], a native of Holland, appeared at the *maison de tolérance* No. 1 [a brothel that Vincent had visited], asked for a girl called Rachel, and handed her his ear with these words: 'Keep this object like a treasure.' Then he disappeared. The police, informed of these events, which could only be the work of an unfortunate madman, looked the next morning for this individual, whom they found in bed with scarcely a sign of life."

Gauguin immediately telegraphed Theo, who arrived in Arles late on Christmas Eve. Theo had long supported his older brother, both financially and emotionally, and he was understandably distraught at Vincent's condition. "He had, while I was with him, moments in which he acted normally, but then after a short while he slipped off into wanderings on philosophy and theology," Theo wrote to his fiancée Johanna Bonger. "It was deeply saddening to witness all this, for from time to time he became conscious of his illness and in those moments he tried to cry—yet no tears came. Poor fighter and poor, poor sufferer. . . . If he had been able to find somebody to whom he could have opened his heart, maybe it would never have come to all

this." A day later, he wrote to Johanna again. "There is little hope, but during his life he has done more than many others, and he has suffered and struggled more than most people could have done. If it must be that he dies, so be it, but my heart breaks when I think of it."

In the end, van Gogh recovered from the attack. In January, he even documented his self-inflicted wound in *Self-Portrait with Bandaged Ear* (see page 68). Apparently considering there was not much he could do for his brother, Theo returned within several days to Paris with Gauguin. Van Gogh remained in the care of Dr. Rey, who wrote to Theo on December 29 that his patient had tried to take a

Shortly after arriving in Arles, Paul Gauguin did this portrait of van Gogh painting his beloved sunflowers. According to Gauguin's memoirs, van Gogh said of the painting, "It is certainly I, but it's I gone mad."

bath in a coal scuttle, had threatened a nurse, and had taken to another patient's bed and refused to budge. His mental state was precarious, the doctor said, and he had to be confined. Yet three days later, van Gogh himself took pen to paper, writing to Theo that he expected to start work again soon, and to Gauguin upbraiding him for causing his brother so much trouble: "Look here—was my brother Theo's journey really necessary, old man? Now at least do reassure him completely, and I entreat you, be confident yourself that after all no evil exists in this best of worlds in which everything is for the best."

In these words, van Gogh summed up his philosophy on life, a philosophy that now, as it had many times in the past, carried him through the greatest difficulties. It was a steadfast belief that the world was inherently good, and that, despite appearances, everything turned out for the best. Van Gogh borrowed his code of principles from the 18th-century novel *Candide,* by Voltaire, in which one of the characters, a preacher named Pangloss, insists, despite continual disasters, that "all is for the best in this best of all possible worlds." Van Gogh, in his naive idealism, did not recognize the irony with which Voltaire drew the ludicrously optimistic character of Father Pangloss. "You don't know the arguments of the good Father Pangloss in Voltaire's *Candide,"* he wrote later to his sister Wilhelmina in Holland while he was in the hospital. "But the memory of them often sustains me in the hours and days and nights that are hardly easy or enviable."

Within a few weeks after his seizure, van Gogh was back at work, with no signs of the illness that had struck him down so severely. Indeed, he tried to pass the episode off as insignificant. "I hope that I have just had simply an artist's fit," he wrote to Theo. "My appetite came back at once, my digestion is all right and my blood recovers from day to day, and in the same way serenity returns. . . . So please quite deliberately forget your unhappy journey and my illness."

But madness was to return periodically for the next year and a half, until July 1890, when a final attack prompted van Gogh to take his own life. In between the bouts, however, he was lucid and highly creative, producing some of his finest works even as he recovered in Saint-Rémy, the mental hospital near Arles in which he had asked Theo to have him confined in May 1889, on the condition that he could continue to paint. To this day, theories abound about the true nature of van Gogh's illness. Epilepsy, manic depression, acute intermittent porphyria, and paranoid schizophrenia have all been advanced as possible causes. Perhaps the best description comes from one Dr. G. Kraus, who, after considering and rejecting a number of hypotheses, declared simply that van Gogh "was an individual in his illness, as well as in his art."

Anna Cornelia Carbentus van Gogh, Vincent's mother, was raised in The Hague and married clergyman Theodorus van Gogh in 1851. Anna had a vibrant personality and enjoyed drawing still lifes of wildflowers. Vincent painted this portrait of his mother in 1888.

2

BOYHOOD
IN BRABANT

VINCENT WILLEM VAN GOGH was born on March 30, 1853, in Groot Zundert, Holland. "Great" Zundert was anything but great, being a tiny hamlet in the largely agricultural region of southern Holland known as Brabant. The adjective probably referred to the wide-open landscape. Here, in the largely Catholic Brabant, van Gogh was born into a Protestant clergyman's family.

Van Gogh's ancestors on both sides were of Dutch bourgeois stock, the kind of well-dressed, stolid-looking people seen in numerous Dutch portraits of the day. His father, Theodorus van Gogh, was one of 12 children born to Pastor Vincent van Gogh of The Hague, Holland's principal administrative center. His mother, Anna Cornelia Carbentus, also came from a well-established family in The Hague. The van Gogh and Carbentus families settled on professions that could not be more disparate. Two of Vincent's maternal aunts married military men who

27

became generals; one of his father's brothers, a vice admiral, served as commandant of the navy yard in Amsterdam, the country's large port city. Three other paternal uncles—fortuitously for the young Vincent—became successful art dealers. And Vincent's father, Theodorus, followed in his own father's footsteps by joining the clergy.

Theodorus was a reserved, intellectual man, who led a life of quiet yet passionate devotion to his family and flock. Throughout his 36-year ministry, he moved from one tiny parish to the next in Brabant, serving as a pastor in the

Theodorus van Gogh, Vincent's father, served as a pastor in the Dutch Reformed church and moved often from one small parish to the next in the Brabant region of Holland. He was an aloof but tolerant parent to the young Vincent.

Dutch Reformed Church, the largest Protestant church in Holland. What he lacked in inspiration as a preacher, Theodorus made up for in steadfastness and tolerance, striving always to find the "middle way," even with Vincent, who often proved to be obstinate. Theodorus's understanding nature can be seen in his face, a good-looking one for which the pastor earned the nickname "handsome Dominie."

Vincent's mother, Anna, was a good counterbalance to her introspective husband. She was vivacious, and an amateur artist of no small talent, who, like Vincent in later life, loved to create still lifes of flowers, including pencil drawings of wildflowers and watercolors of carefully arranged bouquets. As different as his mother and father were, and as radically different as Vincent was from them, both parents exerted a strong influence on their son, who would spend years as an aspiring preacher before finally abandoning the cause only 10 years before his untimely death to become an artist.

Theodorus and Anna married in 1851 and settled into the presbytery on Zundert's main street. The presbytery was a large, two-storied house built in Dutch classical style with a scalloped roofline and a steeply pitched roof, not unlike houses still seen today along the canals and streets of many Dutch towns. Here the pair raised six children. Vincent was born in 1853, followed by Anna in 1855; Theodorus, called Theo, in 1857; Elisabeth in 1859; Wilhelmina in 1862; and Cornelius in 1867. (Ultimately, the sisters would prove of hardier stock: all three lived into their seventies, while their three brothers all died in their thirties.)

Curiously, Vincent almost had an older brother who was given the name Vincent Willem first. On March 30, 1852, a year to the day before Vincent was born, Anna had a stillborn boy. Theodorus and Anna named the dead baby Vincent Willem and buried him in the church graveyard with a stone bearing that name. When Vincent was born a

A photograph taken in 1900 shows the Groot Zundert house (center) in which Vincent was born on March 30, 1853.

year later, they bestowed the same name on him. Every Sunday as he entered the church where his father preached, Vincent passed by a gravestone bearing his own name. Some van Gogh scholars have speculated that Vincent's lifelong soul-searching and his lack of self-confidence can be traced to a feeling of merely being a replacement for someone else. What impact his dead brother had on Vincent and his later mental trouble, however, remains only conjecture.

In truth, in his early years Vincent showed few signs of madness—or, for that matter, of genius. He was a normal child who loved to invent games and to collect objects in the fields and woods around Zundert. His sister Elisabeth later recalled that he would pore over things he found, such as beetles and birds' nests, with the concentration of a naturalist. Vincent's love of nature manifested itself throughout his life, when he lived close to the land as a rural preacher in Holland and later as he took his easel and brushes and headed out-of-doors to paint, often from early morning to well past sunset. Much later, while in the throes of his greatest mental crises, he would remember with an almost hallucinatory clarity Brabant's lonely moors and trim cottages with their tiny gardens. "There will always remain within us something of the Brabant fields and heath," he declared later to his brother Theo.

If any sign at all can be discerned for his later behavior, it was in his intensity. A photograph of Vincent at age 13 shows a freckled, tousle-haired youth with pale, penetrating eyes and a stern expression. In the picture he looks wary, as if a sharp remark could make him start. The young Vincent was prone to stubbornness and unpredictable behavior. When his parents praised him for two early creations—a small elephant crafted in clay and a striking sketch of a cat—Vincent inexplicably destroyed them.

In general, however, Vincent channeled such intensity into intellectual pursuits. Although he inherited none of his father's good looks—those went to his brother Theo—Vincent did have his father's predilection for the life of the mind. Intellectually, he seemed so far beyond the farm boys with whom he attended school in Zundert that his parents pulled him from the school and taught him at home for two years. When he was 11 years old, they sent him to a Protestant boarding school in the nearby village of Zevenbergen. The school's teachers, Jan Provily and his son Piet, kindled Vincent's lifelong passion for languages. Eventually, he would learn to write in English and French almost as well as in his native Dutch, and he came to have a working knowledge of German as well. At the school, Vincent also discovered another passion: reading. In later years, he read widely, from religious tracts to contemporary novels to poetry.

In 1866, Vincent was sent to the King Willem II State Secondary School in Tilburg, and there he got his first taste of the world of art. The school officials prided themselves on maintaining a high academic standard, and they broke the mold of coexistent Dutch schools by devoting four hours per week to art class. The school had managed to hire a capable and forward-thinking artist named C. C. Huysmans, who introduced his students to the exciting new landscapes of the Barbizon painters. Named for the village Barbizon in the Forest of Fontainebleau near Paris where the movement got its start, the Barbizon artists painted directly from nature. Including such artists as Théodore Rousseau and Charles-François Daubigny, the Barbizon painters rejected the high-minded classical and religious themes taught at the large art academies in favor of simpler scenes of everyday life, such as peasants harvesting grain or boats making their way down a river. Daubigny, for example, painted entirely out-of-doors, and his landscapes, according to art critic John Canaday, are "simple poetry . . . [and] intimate." The Barbizon artists' style was lighter, their brushstrokes were freer, and their attitude was a breath of fresh air after decades of stilted academic proselytizing. Vincent, the nature lover and budding artist, was primed for this training and did very well his first year at King Willem.

In March 1868, however, midway through his second year at King Willem, Vincent suddenly quit school, never to return. Why did he leave, especially when things seemed to be going so well? Could his parents no longer afford it? This seems unlikely, because Vincent's Uncle Vincent, a well-to-do art dealer who had no children of his own, had never hesitated—and never would later—to lend a financial hand to the nephew who was his namesake. Did Vincent suffer an early bout of the debilitating illness that would later take such a tragic toll on his life? Probably no one will ever know the reason for his departure, but surely the abrupt end to the studies he cherished left lasting emotional scars.

For a year, Vincent did little but mope about the fields around Zundert. His sister Elisabeth, in a book she wrote years later, remembered him during this period as "broad as he was long, his back slightly bent, with the bad habit of letting his head hang; the red blond hair cropped close was hidden under a straw hat: a strange face, not young; the forehead already full of lines, the eyebrows on the large, noble brow drawn together in deepest thought. The eyes, small and deep-set, were now blue, now green, according to the impression of the moment."

In the summer of 1869, after more than a year of such idleness, Vincent landed his first job. Actually, it was Uncle Cent (short for Vincent) who came through for him, creating an apprentice clerk position for him at Goupil and Company, the gallery Cent worked for in The Hague. Vincent was now 16 years old and would spend the next six years of his life training to become an art dealer.

Vincent van Gogh is seen here in a photograph taken around the year 1872.
At the age of 16, Vincent began his professional life in The Hague at Goupil's,
the gallery in which his uncle Cent had started his own career.

3

ART DEALER

FOR ONE WHO WOULD soon become one of the most radical artists of his day, it is ironic that Vincent, at 16, should begin his professional life working for a highly conservative art gallery specializing in fine reproductions of academic paintings. It was precisely this "old order" that he would soon reject with a vengeance.

Yet Goupil and Company, the gallery he joined in 1869 as an apprentice clerk, proved a solid introduction to the world of art. The gallery was a respectable house with offices in Paris, London, Brussels, and The Hague, to which Vincent was posted. Uncle Cent had made his career at The Hague branch, rising into its top ranks, so it was only fitting that his nephew, just starting his own career in the business, should begin there. Vincent boarded with his parents' friends, the Roos family, who lived along the Lange Beestenmarkt, a street of middle-class houses a short walk from the town center and his office.

As with most things he put his mind to, Vincent threw himself into his new career with enthusiasm. He was put in charge of photographic reproductions at the gallery, and he quickly became adept at convincing customers to buy. He told his brother Theo that he once sold a hundred of the high-quality prints in a single day. To the blossoming artist, the reproductions provided a crash course in the history of art. To flesh out this understanding, van Gogh took to visiting the nearby Mauritshuis, a museum that housed the Dutch royal art collection. Here he got a glimpse of the finest Dutch artists of the past, including the 17th-century masters Rembrandt Harmensz van Rijn, Peter Paul Rubens, Jacob van Ruisdael, and Jan Vermeer.

As fortune would have it, The Hague also proved a good place for Vincent to learn more about the new painting-from-nature style. Even though Uncle Cent worked for a conservative gallery, his personal dream was to create a "school," or group of painters, working in the new movement in his native country of Holland. What better place to establish the new school than in the seat of government of what had recently become the independent kingdom of the Netherlands? Artists would be drawn to The Hague, Cent reasoned, because the town was small and gave quick access to nearby dunes and the sea—ideal conditions for painters to capture the changing light and tones of nature.

Cent's plan worked to a degree. Several prominent nature painters moved there, including Jozef Israëls, who was described as "Millet with color" (Jean-François Millet was one of the leading French painters working in the new natural style), and Anton Mauve. Then only 32 years old, Mauve served as the unofficial conscience of the new school, whose members looked for inspiration back to Rembrandt (who had mastered the use of a freer brush-stroke) and Vermeer (whose paintings perfectly capture light streaming through an open window). Vincent met Mauve, who became his cousin by marriage, in the summer of 1870, and despite Vincent's young age, the two became friends. Mauve was intellectual, forward thinking, and, like Vincent in later years, prone to bouts of melancholia. After Vincent left The Hague in 1873, the two kept in touch, and, in the early 1880s when Vincent finally decided to become an artist, it was Mauve who would teach him oil painting.

For now, however, Vincent's future, as far as he knew, lay in dealing art. He began traveling farther afield to look at artwork, both historical and contemporary. He went to

Anton Mauve painted this self-portrait around the year 1884. Mauve, who befriended van Gogh in 1870 and years later taught him how to paint in oil, was a leading Dutch artist of landscapes and peasant scenes.

Amsterdam to see paintings in the Trippenhuis, the predecessor to the Rijksmuseum, today the country's leading art museum. In July 1872, at age 19, he took his first trip abroad, making his way to Brussels, the capital of Belgium, to attend the annual art show known as the Salon. Like the larger Salon that took place in Paris every year, the Brussels show by then had begun to exhibit, besides the standard academic paintings, works by artists then considered by most to be avant-garde (a group that develops new or experimental techniques). At the 1872 show, Vincent for the first time saw works by such renegade painters as Edouard Manet and Claude Monet.

That summer also marked for Vincent the beginning of a friendship that would sustain him both emotionally and financially throughout his life and result in one of the most heartfelt and historically valuable correspondences in the history of art. The friendship was with his younger brother Theo. Then 15 years old, Theo would finish school in another year. Uncle Cent, thinking how well Vincent had done at Goupil's, convinced Theodorus that Theo should perhaps follow in his older brother's footsteps. So the family sent Theo to stay with Vincent in The Hague that summer to get a taste of living and working in the city.

When Theo left at the end of the summer, Vincent sent him a short note, which launched what would become an 18-year correspondence between the brothers. Just 36 of Theo's letters to Vincent survive, but Theo—and after Theo's death, his wife, Johanna—carefully preserved 670 of Vincent's letters. Often featuring numerous pencil-and-ink sketches, the letters reveal Vincent's innermost thoughts as he struggled to come to terms with himself, his religious beliefs, and his thoughts on art. In some cases, art historians know exactly what Vincent was feeling as he executed a particular painting. Through his letters, Vincent, an emotive and powerful writer, unwittingly produced one of the finest autobiographies of a major artist.

The letters reveal that Vincent initially took on the role of the protective older brother. Soon after Theo arrived in Brussels to take up his new apprentice position at that city's Goupil's branch, Vincent wrote to him, "Don't lose heart if it is very difficult at times; everything will turn out all right. Nobody can do as he wishes at the beginning." Before long, however, the brothers would unconsciously switch roles. Theo would go on to become a successful dealer who, year after year, provided unconditional emotional and financial support to his brother as he struggled to become an artist. Throughout his life, Vincent relied on his family's help (Vincent's father never really approved of his chosen profession and over the years sporadically assisted Vincent financially), but without Theo's selfless and undying support (and the endeavors of Theo's wife after his death), it is not an exaggeration to say that Vincent van Gogh might not be a household name today.

In the meantime, however, Vincent was doing just fine on his own. He had performed so well in his four years at Goupil's that in mid-May 1873 he was promoted to the company's offices in London. Again he was put in charge of the photographic reproduction section, for which he was paid the handsome salary of £90 per year. He moved into the house of a widowed Frenchwoman named Ursula Loyer, who, with her 19-year-old daughter, Eugénie, ran a small day school. "I now have a room such as I always longed for, without a slanting ceiling and without blue paper with a green border," he wrote to Theo, referring obliquely to the cramped attic room he had occupied in his family's home in Zundert. "I live with a very amusing family now; they keep a school for little boys." For nine months, things went swimmingly for Vincent, who was able to improve his English and had enough money to enjoy the city, then the industrial capital of the world.

But then a disastrous thing happened: he fell in love with his landlady's daughter. It was not the act of falling in love with Eugénie that proved calamitous, but the fact that, over the nine months that his love steadily grew, Vincent never once let his feelings be known to her. At the time, Vincent's only understanding of the ways of the heart came from a book titled simply *L'Amour* (Love). The fact that the book had been written not by a romantic writer or poet but by a historian, Jules Michelet, should perhaps have given him pause. But he fell for its advice completely. Essentially, the book led him to believe that love just happened, that he should wait patiently until, at some unforeseen moment, he and Eugénie simply came together as lovers. Eventually, however, the strain proved too great, and one day Vincent expressed his love. To his utter shock, Eugénie spurned him, saying she was secretly engaged to be married to another man.

Vincent took the rejection about as hard as anyone could have. He immediately left the Loyers' house, abandoning all his belongings and moving into cheap lodgings, and he lost all interest in his work at Goupil's. The event marked the first of several disastrous encounters he would have with women and the beginning of the peculiar behavior for which he increasingly became known. The few letters he sent home said nothing of his unrequited love, but instead contained long biblical quotations and obscure lines of verse—the first signs of a creeping religious fanaticism that would soon take over his life. An uncle visiting London dropped in on Vincent, and his subsequent report to Theodorus and Anna did not reassure them that all was well with their son.

In the early summer, Vincent, looking depressed and disheveled, arrived for a holiday visit at his parents' house in Helviort, where his father was now billeted. But the family was used to strange illnesses—two of Theodorus's brothers constantly complained of ill-defined maladies, and one of Anna's sisters was epileptic—and so they did nothing, thinking that in time Vincent would get over whatever plagued him.

But in the months following his return to London in July, Vincent's situation did not improve. He moved into new lodgings on Kennington New Road near the Loyers' house, perhaps in hopes of eventually winning over Eugénie. But she showed no interest in him. Depressed, he went to a museum in the East End slums, and there he came into contact for the first time with extreme poverty. In the face of such despair, his work as a high-paid art dealer seemed increasingly pointless to him. He became more and more interested in religion, often staying up late reading the Bible.

Claude Monet's notorious Impression: Sunrise *of 1872 supplied the new name for the group of painters who had exhibited their works at the Salon of 1874. Dubbed "impressionists," a nickname that was supposed to mock them, the artists willingly accepted the new label because it described their "painting in terms of tone rather than in terms of the object itself."*

Vincent's lack of enthusiasm did not go unobserved by his employers at Goupil's, and thinking a change of scene might do him good, Uncle Cent arranged in 1874 for him to be transferred to the gallery's main office in Paris. Before he left London, Vincent dispatched a letter to Theo in which he included a quotation from the French historian Ernest Renan that, in essence, would become his personal credo. "Man is not on this earth merely to be happy, nor even to be simply honest. He is there to realize great things for humanity, to attain nobility and to surmount the vulgarity in which the existence of almost all individuals drags on."

Vincent lived in Paris from October to December, and then briefly returned to London, but his colleagues found him increasingly peculiar, and he was sent back to Paris in May 1875. Had he been in a more upbeat frame of mind, Vincent might have been taken with the mood of excitement over the new mode of painting then sweeping avant-garde artistic circles in Paris. The year before, the French capital had hosted a landmark show of the works of painters whose names today are famous the world over but then were all but unknown: Edgar Degas, Claude Monet, Pierre Auguste Renoir, and Berthe Morisot, among others. Most art critics were still shocked by the rough-hewn, sometimes unfinished look and commonplace subjects of the paintings. Monet's 1872 painting *Impression: Sunrise,* the hit of the show among believers, led one derisive critic to dismiss the new artists as little more than a bunch of "impressionists." The name stuck, and today the artists so disparaged at the 1874 show are synonymous with Impressionism, one of the best-loved styles of modern art.

But Vincent had other things on his mind. In his new apartment in Montmartre, the bohemian section of Paris, his roommate, an Englishman and colleague at Goupil's named Harry Gladwell, recalled that Vincent often stayed up late reading the Bible aloud to himself. Vincent's letters to his brother in Brussels, and later The Hague, bore full texts of hymns and other religious quotations that could only have baffled and worried Theo, who was well on his way to becoming one of Europe's leading young art dealers. At Goupil's headquarters in Paris, meanwhile, Vincent began to dissuade customers from purchasing paintings of which he did not approve. Worse still, during the height of the 1875 Christmas rush, Goupil's busiest season, Vincent suddenly left the office without telling his employers and paid a holiday visit to his parents in Etten, Holland, another new parish presided over by Theodorus.

The handwriting was on the wall. When Vincent returned to the office at the beginning of the New Year, his employers were incensed. Knowing what was coming, he asked calmly if there were any complaints against him. When his boss acknowledged that there were, Vincent quietly offered his resignation. Although unable to forestall his nephew's departure, Uncle Cent made it possible for him to continue for another three months, until April 1, 1876. On that day, Vincent's six-year career as an art dealer came to an abrupt end. As he wrote to Theo, "When the apple is ripe, a soft breeze makes it fall from the tree; such as is the case here." For the next four years, Vincent would devote his life to preaching—to a degree that would take a serious and lasting toll on his mental and physical health.

Extremely affected by the misery he observed around him, van Gogh painted Miners' Wives *while living in The Hague in 1882. From 1880 to 1886, van Gogh painted figures overwhelmed by their burdens, professing his excessive preoccupation with the humanitarianism that had led him to become an evangelist.*

4

EVANGELIST

OVER THE NEXT FIVE YEARS, van Gogh would live in five cities in three countries. He was adrift, physically and psychologically, trying to come to terms with himself and the previously unseen world of the poor and despairing, which had so moved him when he first came upon it in London's East End slums. To the consternation of his family and colleagues, he had deliberately put an end to a promising and lucrative career in order to help the destitute. The question he now fought with was, how best to do it?

After resigning from Goupil's, van Gogh returned to London. Although the city had been the scene of his greatest unhappiness, it had also been the site of his first recognition of that nebulous world to which he was so strongly drawn. (He may also have wished to try his chances once again with Eugénie Loyer.) Rapid industrialization throughout the 19th century had left London, the industrial center of the world, with an increasingly clear-cut division between the haves and the have-nots. So although poverty reigned in other cities—indeed, even in the rural villages of van Gogh's native Holland—in London it had a profound effect on the impressionable would-be evangelist.

Van Gogh, however, did not yet know he wanted to be a preacher. He just wanted to help the underprivileged in some way. Through want ads placed in London newspapers, he landed a job as a teacher in a boarding school for boys in Ramsgate, a seaside town on the Strait of Dover. The school's decrepit condition suited his current temperament. Dank and forbidding, the building had cold, dark stairways, broken windows, and hordes of insects. After earning a high salary at Goupil's, van Gogh received only room and board for his efforts, which included teaching elementary mathematics, French, and German. Even a self-chastising van Gogh found the conditions appalling. When the school's owner opened a new school in Isleworth, a town near London, and offered him a position there, he immediately accepted.

At Isleworth, van Gogh got his wish: to preach to the poor. At the school, he taught Bible classes and, through the good graces of the minister at a local Methodist chapel, began preaching his first sermons. His letters home resounded with pedagogical sermonizing. "Do you ever go to Communion?" he asked Theo in the margin of a letter. "They that are whole need not a physician, but they that are sick." He concluded the letter with a fit of near-hysterical ranting. "For I am with thee saith the Lord, to save thee. . . . All thy lovers have forgotten thee. . . . I shall restore health unto thee, and take the plagues away from thee." Van Gogh signed off with three separately quoted lines. "The Lord hath appeared of old to me, saying, Yea, I have loved thee with an everlasting love." "As one whom his mother comforted, so will I comfort you, saith the Lord." "There is a friend that sticketh closer than a brother."

Preoccupied with religious matters, van Gogh began to neglect his physical health. Initially, he deliberately denied himself food, partially to save money, but primarily to punish himself, like a Buddhist hermit. Later, when he was painting full-time, he felt the act of eating interrupted his work and hampered the sense of heightened awareness that he got from taking in only coffee. Van Gogh was a large man who ate frighteningly little. This disregard for simple sustenance eventually shook the foundations of his physical and mental health.

When he went home for the Christmas holidays in 1876, his father was so appalled at his emaciated appearance that he refused to let him return to England. Van Gogh, confused and distraught, agreed. Theodorus again sought the help of his brother, and again Uncle Cent came through, arranging for his nephew to work in a bookstore in Dordrecht, Holland. Van Gogh took up his new position in January.

But van Gogh's heart was no more in selling books than it had been in selling artwork. Years later, the bookstore manager's son recalled that van Gogh spent his working hours secretly translating passages from the Bible from Dutch into French, German, and English, using paper divided into four columns. He also involved himself with his other passion, the manager's son wrote, sketching "silly pen-and-ink drawings, a little tree with a lot of branches and side branches and twigs."

Although the bookstore owner understandably only saw van Gogh's weaknesses—and fired him within four months—van Gogh's roommate in Dordrecht, a young schoolteacher named P. C. Gorlitz, drew a more sympathetic portrait:

> He was a singular man with a singular appearance into the bargain. He was well made, and had reddish hair which stood up on end; his face was homely and covered with freckles, but changed and brightened wonderfully when he warmed into enthusiasm, which happened often

enough. Van Gogh provoked laughter repeatedly by his attitude and behavior—for everything he did and thought and felt, and his way of living, was different from that of others of his age. At table he said lengthy prayers and ate like a penitent friar: for instance, he would not take meat, gravy, etc. And then his face always had an abstracted expression—pondering, deeply serious, melancholy. But when he laughed, he did so heartily and with gusto, and his whole face brightened.

Now 24 years old, van Gogh decided to become a clergyman like his father. Returning to Etten, van Gogh found his parents approving of his idea. They determined that their son should study in Amsterdam and that he should have a private tutor. Acceding again to his father's plans for him, van Gogh moved to the giant port city in May 1877 and immediately received as tutor Dr. Mendes da Costa, a scholar who was not much older than Vincent himself. Though a Jew, da Costa prepared his new student for his Protestant theological-school exams by teaching him Greek and Latin.

Again, van Gogh had trouble applying himself. "After a short time the Greek verbs became too much for him," da Costa wrote in a memoir published in 1910. "However I might set about it, whatever trick I might invent to enliven the lessons, it was no use. 'Mendes,' he would say . . . 'do you seriously believe that such horrors are indispensable to a man who wants to do what I want to do: give peace to poor creatures and reconcile them to their existence here on earth?'" Since he knew that he had to pass the exams if he wanted to be a full-fledged minister, van Gogh tried very hard. But to him, the studies seemed to bear little relation to his plans to help the downtrodden.

To truly understand the poor, and thus be in a position to help them, van Gogh seemed to feel he had to bring himself, physically and socially, to their level in society. How could he know how they suffered if he had not suffered similarly himself? "Whenever Vincent felt that his thoughts had strayed farther than they should have," da Costa recalled, "he took a cudgel [club] to bed with him and belabored his back with it; and whenever he was convinced that he had forfeited the privilege of spending the night in his bed, he slunk out of the house [and slept] on the floor of a little wooden shed, without bed or blanket. He preferred to do this in the winter."

After more than a year of study with Mendes da Costa, van Gogh abruptly terminated their relationship. Perhaps admitting to himself that he was not up to the task of becoming an ordained minister—or not patient enough— he moved to Brussels in August 1878 and enrolled in a training school for lay preachers. Graduates of the program

In one of his earliest drawings, Men and Women Going to the Mines (1880), van Gogh portrays the gloom of hardship with which the men and women of the Borinage had to daily contend. Van Gogh zealously followed the true teachings of Christ while he preached to the poor; he even gave away his bed to someone who was destitute and slept on the floor.

were not ministers, but they could preach the gospel and
do missionary work among the poor. If he did well at the
school, his administrators promised, they might assign
him a mission somewhere in Belgium. But he did not do
well, and for the same reasons he failed with da Costa.
One of his fellow students recalled that when a teacher
asked van Gogh during a grammar lesson which case a
word was, nominative or dative, he responded, "Oh, sir, I
really don't care."

An impatient van Gogh abandoned any further notions
of study and, with what little money his father could give
him, set off around Christmas, 1878, to a poor coal-mining
region of southern Belgium called the Borinage. He could
not have chosen a bleaker place to satiate his desire to help
the oppressed. "Everywhere around one sees the big chim-
neys and the immense heaps of coal at the entrance to the
mines," he wrote to Theo. "Most of the miners are thin and
pale from fever and look tired and emaciated, weather-
beaten and prematurely aged, the women as a whole faded
and worn. Round the mine are poor miners' huts with a
few smoke-blackened dead trees, thorn hedges, dunghills,
ash heaps, slag." Conditions inside the mines, into which
van Gogh descended, were even more depressing. "Imagine a row of cells in a rather narrow, low passage, shored
up with rough timber," he told Theo. "In each of those cells
a miner in a coarse linen suit, filthy and black as a chimney
sweep, is busy hewing coal by the pale light of a small
lamp. The miner can stand erect in some cells; in others he
lies on the ground. The arrangement is more or less like
the cells in a beehive . . . or like the partitions in a crypt."

For a while van Gogh thought he had found his mission
in life. He started a Bible school in a community center
where he preached to the miners and their families. He
helped to care for miners injured in all-too-frequent cave-
ins and explosions and others made ill by the sulfurous
smoke that hung over the region. He drew sketches of
people struggling under the most appalling conditions,

including children loading coal on horse-drawn carts deep within the mines. The missionary society in Brussels was so impressed with his earnest efforts that it bestowed on him a six-month trial appointment as a lay preacher, with a salary of about $10 per month.

But before long it became clear that he had begun to let his missionary fervor get the better of him. He took the precepts of the New Testament too literally, particularly the injunction, "Sell that thou hast, and give it to the poor." He cast off his clothing in favor of a homemade sackcloth shirt and a tattered military tunic, and he left the coal dust on his face, the better to fit in with his begrimed flock. He moved out of the room he had been renting in a baker's house and took to sleeping on the floor of a hut. When the missionary society took issue with his "excessive zeal" and asked him to conduct himself in a more orderly manner, van Gogh refused and was dismissed by the society. He stayed on, however, surviving on what little handouts the miners could spare.

Theo came down from Brussels to reason with him. Dismayed by the almost inhuman state into which his brother had willingly fallen, Theo urged him to take up another profession, perhaps as a baker or an engraver. Theo, now a leading art dealer, intimated that the life Vincent led was merely an excuse for idleness. Van Gogh bristled at the suggestion. "May I observe," he wrote to Theo after his visit, "that this is a rather strange sort of 'idleness'? It is somewhat difficult for me to defend myself, but I should be very sorry if, sooner or later, you could not see it differently."

Van Gogh at least made the effort to go to Brussels and try to get himself reappointed by the missionary society. He took along his portfolio of sketches, which, in the light of events about to take place, can be seen as the harbinger of his imminent journey from religion to art. On his way back to the Borinage—he had failed in his efforts in Brussels—he stayed a few days with his parents in Etten.

Theo van Gogh, Vincent's younger brother, became a high-ranking art dealer at Goupil's and implored Vincent to take up a profession other than evangelism. Theo worried about his brother's state of mind and believed Vincent's way of life in the Borinage was just an excuse for idleness.

His mother recalled that he spent all day reading Charles Dickens's novel *Hard Times.* It must have seemed to van Gogh that, under his present circumstances, the novel had been written specifically with him in mind. The main character, Stephen Blackpool, is just one of many faceless employees working long hours in the textile mills of a dark, highly polluted town named Coketown, whose residents fail to recognize Blackpool's potential.

Upon his return to the Coketown-like Borinage in the fall, van Gogh withdrew into himself. With no income and winter approaching, his prospects seemed as bleak as they could possibly be. For years he had written regularly to

Theo, but the letter he posted on October 15, 1879, was the last he would send for 10 months. It is not known how he managed to survive the winter, either bodily or emotionally, for during that time he seemed to have suffered a severe mental breakdown. When he finally broke his silence the following summer, he referred obliquely to what he had been through. "What molting time is to birds, so adversity or misfortune is . . . for us human beings," he wrote to Theo. "One can stay in it . . . one can also emerge renewed, but it must not be done in public and it is not at all amusing; therefore the only thing to do is to hide oneself. Well, so be it."

By the time he recovered, van Gogh had decided to become an artist.

The Potato Eaters, *van Gogh's homage to the suffering peasants, is considered by most art historians to be his first masterpiece. He completed the canvas, painted in depressing browns and greenish blacks, in April 1885, shortly after his father's death in Nuenen.*

5

THE POTATO EATERS

IN THE DEPTHS of that gruesome winter, van Gogh decided he had to pay a visit to Jules Breton, a French poet and painter he had met at Goupil's. Breton lived in the village of Courrières, about 45 miles from the Borinage coal mines where van Gogh lived. Because he had only 10 francs to his name, van Gogh had no choice but to make the journey on foot. Someone else might have thought better of it in such conditions. But van Gogh was on a mission. It was a mission that even he could not have explained, but in hindsight it can be seen symbolically as his first attempt to shed the preacher's habit and assume the artist's mantle.

With no money to stay at an inn, van Gogh was forced to spend nights outside in the bitter cold. Later, when he had resumed writing to Theo, he recalled that he had slept "once in an abandoned wagon, which was white with frost the next morning—rather a bad resting place; once in a pile of faggots [bundles of sticks]; and one time that was a little better, in a haystack, where I succeeded in making a rather more comfortable berth—but then a drizzling rain did not exactly further my well-being."

When he finally arrived at Breton's studio, something about the "Methodist regularity" of the studio intimidated him, and he could not bring himself to knock on the door. Having come all that way, another person would likely have fairly burst through the door. But van Gogh turned around and walked back to the Borinage, never having laid eyes on Breton. He stumbled back into his tumbledown quarters at the coal mines "overcome by fatigue, with sore feet, and quite melancholy."

But forces were at work within him. Even as he despaired, he felt energy well up within him and, he declared to Theo, "I said to myself, in spite of everything I shall rise again: I will take up my pencil, which I have forsaken in my great discouragement, and I will go on with my drawing. From that moment everything has seemed transformed for me, and I will go on."

By the summer, van Gogh had indeed transformed himself. He had passed through a self-inflicted purgatory and reached a sort of enlightenment, one that combined his fervid religious beliefs with his blossoming notions about art. "I think that everything which is really good and beautiful—of inner moral, spiritual and sublime beauty in men and their works—comes from God, and that all which is bad and wrong in men and their works is not of God, and God does not approve of it," he wrote to Theo in July 1880. "To give you an example: someone loves Rembrandt, but seriously—that man will know there is a God, he will surely believe it. . . . To try to understand the real significance of what the great artists, the serious masters, tell us in their masterpieces, that leads to God; one man wrote or told it in a book; another, in a picture."

Van Gogh, of course, would tell it in pictures. He had finally found his mission in life. His letters now show an assuredness heretofore unknown, a confidence in the rightness of his decision to become an artist. "Strangely enough, I sometimes make small sketches almost against my will," he confessed to Theo. He drew many of them in the margins of letters he sent to Theo, who, by carefully preserving the letters, also preserved sketches that reveal the artist in the very midst of perfecting his craft. In another, later letter to his brother, van Gogh wrote, "If you hear a voice within you saying, 'You are not a painter,' *then by all means paint,* boy, and that voice will be silenced, but only by working. . . . One must undertake [work] with confidence, with a certain assurance that one is doing a reasonable thing, like the farmer who drives his plow."

Van Gogh now had that assurance, and he used it as the platform from which to launch one of the most remarkable careers in painting—remarkable for its brevity, intensity, and unparalleled accomplishments. In the summer, he opened his first studio in a coal miner's cottage in the Borinage and began copying prints that Theo sent him. At age 27, he was getting a late start in art, with most artists at his level many years younger. So he decided with characteristic determination to make up for lost time. In the next several years, he drew hundreds of detailed studies and copied the works of old masters and contemporary artists alike.

In October 1880, he left the Borinage for Brussels. Although his artistic drive would soon prove unstoppable, he clearly still had some moments of doubt as to his ability and his future. As he left he told the pastor with whom he had worked there, "Nobody has understood me. They think I'm a madman because I wanted to be a true Christian. They turned me out like a dog, saying that I was causing a scandal, because I tried to relieve the misery of the wretched. I don't know what I'm going to do. Perhaps you are right, and I am idle and useless on this earth."

Though he had no specific plan for what he would do in the Belgian capital, van Gogh was now receiving 60 francs per month from his father, and that money gave him the confidence to make a fresh start. (That winter, when the monthly stipend was raised to 100 francs, he learned that the money had come all along from Theo, who, in the two years he had worked at Goupil's in Paris, had risen to a prominent position despite his young age.) In Brussels, van Gogh rented the cheapest hotel room he could find. He continued sketching and rendering existing works in his copybooks, and he began taking drawing lessons from a young painter named Anton van Rappard.

As usual, however, he neglected his health. This was due in part to lack of funds—50 of the 60 francs he received when he first arrived in Brussels went to his monthly rent. But increasingly it was because of his preoccupation with work and the view that he needed only the most minimal sustenance to keep up. While in Brussels, he wrote to Theo that "my chief food is dry bread and some potatoes or chestnuts which people sell here on the street corners." In another letter, he admitted that at one point he had "lived mainly for four days on 23 cups of coffee."

His perpetual lack of money drove him, in April 1881, to move in with his parents in Etten. He told Theo that he expected Theodorus and Anna to misunderstand him. "I blame no one for it," he asserted, "because relatively few people know why an artist acts as he does."

Nor, he would prove, why a lover acts as he does. In Etten, van Gogh fell in love for a second time, with an outcome just as unfortunate as that with Eugénie Loyer in England. This time, the target of his affections was his first cousin, Kee Vos, a young widow with a four-year-old son. Never one to come straight out with his feelings, van Gogh initially endeared himself to the boy in hopes of winning over his mother. But when Vos failed to show any interest, he screwed up his courage and declared his love for her. Startled, she calmly replied that she never planned to marry again. When he pressed her, she backed off, crying, "No, never, never!"

Van Gogh, with his usual dogged determination, would not take no for an answer, so Vos fled to the home of her parents, Anna's sister and her husband, in Amsterdam.

Undaunted, van Gogh continued to write to her. He explained to Theo that "love is something so positive, so strong, so real that it is as impossible for one who loves to take back that feeling as it is to take his own life." Such a force drove him to follow Vos to Amsterdam, with catastrophic results. His letters are vague on the subject, but when he arrived at his relatives' house and was told by his aunt and uncle that he could not see their daughter, van Gogh apparently stuck his hand into the flame of a lamp and said he would talk to her only so long as he could endure the pain. Dumbstruck, Vos's parents blew out the lamp, and, van Gogh recalled later, "everything became a blank." When he came to, his aunt and uncle helped him to his feet. "And, dear me, those two old people went with me through the cold, foggy, muddy streets and they did indeed show me a very good, cheap inn."

On his way back to Etten (he never did see his cousin), van Gogh stopped in The Hague, where, in a kind of retaliation, he paid a visit to a prostitute, Christien Clasina Maria Hoornik, who also posed as a model for him. "And we talked about everything, about her life, about her cares, about her misery, about her health, and with her I had a more interesting conversation than, for instance, with my very learned, professorial cousin," he wrote to Theo, referring to his cousin-by-marriage, the painter Anton Mauve. He admitted that the streetwalker was no substitute for his real love Kee Vos, but claimed that "I need a woman, I cannot, I will not live without love. I am a man and a man with passions. I must go to a woman, otherwise I shall freeze or turn to stone."

Van Gogh's failure in love coincided with his loss of faith in the organized church, in which until recently he had believed so fervently. Ironically, he chose Christmas Day in Etten to denounce the church to his father, who, of

Van Gogh drew Behind the Schenkweg *in May 1882 after he returned to The Hague to live. He wrote to his brother around this time, explaining, "Theo, I am definitely not a landscape painter; when I make landscapes, there will always be something of the figure in them."*

course, had devoted his life to it. In a letter, van Gogh told Theo that he had told Theodorus "straight out that I considered the whole system abominable." Theo, for once, was furious with his brother. "That you could not bear it there any longer is possible," he fired back, "and that you differ in opinion with people who have lived all their lives in the country and have not come in contact with modern life is not unnatural; but, confound it, what made you so childish and impudent as to embitter and spoil Father's and Mother's life in that way?"

Van Gogh would not stop there. Railing against his parents' bourgeois lifestyle, in which people, he complained to Theo, "attach importance to refinement and outward form," van Gogh returned to The Hague shortly after Christmas and took up again with the prostitute. Christien Hoornik, whom van Gogh called Sien, was the antithesis of the refined Kee Vos. A prostitute for half of her 30 years, Sien spoke crudely, smoked cigars, and drank heavily. She had one illegitimate child and was pregnant with another. Her face was pitted from smallpox, and she suffered from gonorrhea (an infectious, sexually transmitted disease), which she would soon give to van Gogh.

Despite his own indigence, van Gogh began paying her rent, "and thank God, so far I have been able to protect her and her child from hunger and cold by sharing my own bread with her," he wrote Theo. "It seems to me that every man worth a straw would have done the same in such a case." He even planned to marry her. "I can only marry once, and how can I do better than marry her?" he asked his brother rhetorically. "It is the only way to help her; otherwise misery would force her back into her old ways, which end in a precipice."

Sien inspired his 1882 drawing *Sorrow,* which van Gogh recreated in a lithograph. The work shows the compassion he had for his companion in the way he depicts sadness and human tragedy in the dejected, hunched nude female figure. In the end, however, van Gogh never did marry Sien, and after living together for about a year and a half, the two parted ways. But by taking up with a woman who, because of her wretched circumstances, could not afford to refuse his advances, van Gogh showed how frustrated he had become in failing to find someone with whom he could truly open his heart.

Never again would he become involved with a woman; from now on, his work became his all-consuming passion. Indeed, all the feelings that he could not share with a woman he intended to share with viewers of his artwork. Shortly after moving to The Hague in the winter of 1881–82, he wrote a letter to Theo in which he declared his mission as an artist:

> I want you to understand clearly my conception of art.
> What I want and aim at is confoundedly difficult, and yet
> I do not think I aim too high. I want to do drawings which

touch some people. . . . In either figure or landscape I should wish to express, not sentimental melancholy, but serious sorrow. . . . I want to progress so far that people will say of my work, he feels deeply, he feels tenderly—notwithstanding my so-called roughness, perhaps even because of it. . . . What am I in most people's eyes? A nonentity, or an eccentric and disagreeable man—somebody who has no position in society and never will have, in short, the lowest of the low. Very well . . . then I should want my work to show what is in the heart of such an eccentric, of such a nobody. This is my ambition, which is, in spite of everything, founded less on anger than on love.

After a life of false starts, van Gogh was finally underway as a professional artist. In The Hague, he placed himself under the tutelage of Anton Mauve, who taught him the fundamentals of painting in oils. Van Gogh would be dead in less than 10 years, but in that time, he not only mastered oil painting, but developed one of the most striking and most easily recognizable styles in modern art. His manner of painting featured a heavy impasto style, with globs of paint formed like clay on the canvas. Van Gogh became so liberal with paint that in certain works ridges of pigment rose a full inch off the canvas. In an August 1882 letter to Theo, van Gogh reveals the exact moment he discovered the technique, which became one of his trademarks:

In the woods, yesterday toward evening I was busy painting a rather sloping ground covered with dry, moldered beech leaves. This ground was light and dark reddish-brown, made more so by the shadows of trees casting more or less dark streaks over it, sometimes half blotted out. The problem was—and I found it very difficult—to get the depth of color, the enormous force and solidity of that ground. . . . It struck me how sturdily those little [sapling] stems were rooted in the ground. I began painting them with a brush, but because the surface was already so heavily covered, a brush stroke was lost in it—then I

squeezed the roots and trunks in from the tube, and mod-
eled it a little with the brush. Yes—now they stand there
rising from the ground, strongly rooted in it. . . . In a certain
way I am glad that I have not *learned* painting, because
then I might have *learned* to pass by such effects as this.

Van Gogh also began using a technique that simplified
the business of working perspective (the illusion of
three-dimensionality) into a painting. The device was
simply a wooden frame with four threads stretched
across it—two diagonally from the corners and one each
straight across from the middle point of all four sides—so
that they all met in the middle. "The lines of roofs and
gutters now come shooting forth powerfully, like arrows
from a bow," van Gogh wrote of the drawings he created
using the frame. Van Gogh's deeply foreshortened perspective, resulting in his later paintings in roads that seem
impossibly steep and farm fields that tilt unnaturally forward toward the viewer, became as much a trademark of
his artwork as his impasto style.

These stylistic breakthroughs were significant in van
Gogh's eyes only insofar as they could help him express
the strong emotions of sympathy and understanding he felt
for people and the natural world. To get closer to the land
and the peasants he loved so passionately, van Gogh left
The Hague in September 1883 for Drenthe, a province in
the peat-bog region of northern Holland. He was following
in the footsteps of his erstwhile teachers van Rappard and
Mauve, who had also gone to the pastoral region to get
closer to nature.

Van Gogh lasted only three months in Drenthe. He
lacked sufficient painting materials, felt guilty about having abandoned Sien, and found the peasants he had traveled so far to paint unwilling to pose for him. Not
untypically, he left on the spur of the moment, taking only
a few paintings with him and leaving a large body of work
behind. (Years later, it was revealed that the owners of the
room he had rented—and where he abandoned his work—

had given away the works as Christmas presents, until one year when the owners' daughter took the remaining drawings and paintings and, one by one, crammed them into a burning stove.)

As he had done several times in the past, van Gogh moved back in with his parents, who now lived in Nuenen, Holland. In a letter to his brother in Paris, he imagined how he must have appeared to his parents when he unexpectedly arrived at the house in Nuenen in the late fall, unkempt and emaciated. "They feel the same dread about taking me into the house as they would about taking a big rough dog. He would run into the room with wet paws—and he is so rough. He will be in everyone's way. And he barks so loud. In short, he is a foul beast." But his parents' way had always been one of forbearance and conciliation. Theodorus helped his prodigal son set up a studio in an unused laundry room, writing to Theo that "we undertake this experiment with real confidence and we intend to leave him perfectly free in his peculiarities of dress etc."

The experiment worked better than anyone could have expected, least of all van Gogh himself. He stayed nearly two years, furiously producing still lifes, landscapes, and scenes of peasants at work. In the first seven months of 1884 alone, van Gogh executed 10 paintings and 17 drawings and watercolors of Nuenen weavers, who sat alone for untold hours working their looms. "The miners and the weavers still constitute a race apart from other laborers and artisans, and I feel a great sympathy for them," van Gogh wrote. "With his dreamy air . . . almost a sleepwalker—that is the weaver." All told, van Gogh produced during his stay in Nuenen a corpus of work that included more than 280 drawings and watercolors and nearly as many oil paintings.

Van Gogh was so preoccupied with his work that two personal tragedies that occurred during his sojourn at Nuenen barely landed even glancing blows on him. First, a 41-year-old woman named Margot Begemann fell in

(continued on page 73)

Selected Paintings by
VINCENT VAN GOGH

Fritillaries. Oil on canvas, 1887.

Gypsy Camp. Oil on canvas, 1888.

The Bridge at Langlois. Oil on canvas, 1888.

Self-Portrait with Bandaged Ear. Oil on canvas, 1889.

The Postman Roulin. Oil on canvas, 1889.

Daubigny's Garden.
Oil on canvas, 1890.

le jardin de Daubigny

The Starry Night. Oil on canvas, 1889.

(continued from page 64)

love with Vincent, the only woman ever to do so. In a strange role reversal for him, van Gogh spurned her advances. One day, while the two were walking near Nuenen, Begemann collapsed in a convulsive fit. Van Gogh carried her back to her home, where she was administered an emetic that brought up most of what she had taken—the poison strychnine. Begemann survived, and her parents put her under the care of a physician in Utrecht.

The second tragedy concerned Theodorus. On March 24, 1885, Theodorus had written to Theo of his ongoing frustration at being unable to communicate with his oldest son. "May he meet with success in something, no matter what," Theodorus wrote, almost by way of a parting prayer. Two days later, he collapsed on the front stoop of his house and died. He was 63 years old. In a letter to his brother Theo shortly thereafter, van Gogh, who had never been close to Theodorus, only briefly mentioned his father's passing before going into detail about his plans to do a painting of "peasants around a dish of potatoes in the evening."

Van Gogh's watercolor The Weaver *(January 1884) illustrates the artist's fascination with the weaver and his loom. Van Gogh once said that if a person compared his depiction with one done by a mechanic, in his "you could not help thinking occasionally of the workman, whereas absolutely nothing like it would occur to your mind when you looked at the model of a loom drawn by a mechanic."*

The painting that resulted, *The Potato Eaters* (1885), is widely considered van Gogh's first masterpiece. It shows a family of peasants crowded around a crude table lit by a single lamp, eating their evening meal. "I have tried to emphasize that these people, eating their potatoes in the lamplight, have dug the earth with those very hands they put in the dish, and so it speaks of *manual labor,* and how they have honestly earned their food," van Gogh explained to Theo. "I have wanted to give the impression of a way of life quite different from that of us civilized people. . . . I think a peasant girl is more beautiful than a lady, in her dusty, patched blue skirt and bodice. . . . If a peasant picture smells of bacon, smoke, potato steam—all right, that's not unhealthy; if a stable smells of dung—all right, that belongs to a stable; if the field has an odor of ripe corn or potatoes or of guano [bird droppings used as fertilizer] or manure—that's healthy."

Proud of his achievement, van Gogh sent a lithograph of the painting to van Rappard in The Hague. But the praise he longed for—and expected—was not forthcoming. "You will agree with me that such work is not meant seriously," van Rappard wrote back about *The Potato Eaters.* "Fortunately you can do better than that, but why then did you see and treat everything so superficially?" Van Rappard fired off a litany of criticisms, demanding to know why the male figure on the right is not "allowed" to have "a knee, a belly and lungs?" Why, he wondered, "must his arm be a meter too short? And why must he do without half his nose? And why must that woman on the right have some sort of tobacco pipe stem with a little cube on the end for a nose? And after that, while working in such a manner you dare to invoke the names of Millet and Breton. Come on! In my opinion art is too sublime a thing to be treated so nonchalantly." Earlier in his career, van Gogh may have suffered inordinately from such criticism. But now he knew better. He simply folded up van Rappard's note and mailed it back to him.

That van Gogh dismissed his former teacher's criticisms out of hand shows how far he had advanced in his art. He had stepped beyond the narrow artistic boundaries that enclosed van Rappard's vision of art. In a letter he sent to Theo after shipping the painting to him in Paris, van Gogh nevertheless unconsciously answered van Rappard's criticisms by stating that "I should be desperate if my figures were correct. . . . I do not want to be academically correct. . . . [F]or me, Millet and Lhermitte [a minor artist of the day] are the real artists for the very reason that they do not paint things as they are, traced in a dry analytical way, but as they . . . feel them . . . my great longing is to learn to make those very incorrectnesses, those deviations, remodelings, changes in reality, so that they may become, yes, lies if you like—but truer to the literal truth."

Theo had no luck in selling the painting, however. He had enough trouble selling Impressionist works—he had sold only three so far in 1885—and Impressionist paintings had received a lot of critical attention, unlike the then-unknown works of Vincent van Gogh. Within a short period of time, van Gogh would become one of the most intense colorists of his day, but for now, his dark, brooding pictures, executed in the subdued hues of browns and greenish blacks then favored by most painters in the Low Countries, could not hold a candle to the brightly colored paintings of the Impressionists. Theo repeatedly advised his brother that, to conform to the modern style and thus to sell paintings, he desperately needed to lighten his palette. But van Gogh, stuck in provincial Holland, had only seen a handful of Impressionist paintings and, in a sense, did not know what color was.

Nevertheless, he began to think obsessively about color. In October 1885, he paid a visit to the new Rijksmuseum in Amsterdam. Though he spent the entire day sitting before a single painting, Rembrandt's *The Jewish Bride* (circa 1665), he wrote to Theo later that his thoughts focused on Peter Paul Rubens, Diego Velázquez, and

Jean-François Millet, a leading Barbizon artist, ennobled peasant life in his 1857 painting The Gleaners *(right). Van Gogh saw Millet's canvas and greatly admired it;* his own *Planting Potatoes of 1884 (opposite) acknowledges the influence of Millet. Some scholars today regard van Gogh as Millet's spiritual son.*

Eugène Delacroix—on color, color, color. He began to realize that his destiny lay beyond Nuenen and beyond the somber paintings he had fashioned for the past five years. When a friend to whom he had given one of his paintings that fall observed that he had forgotten to sign it, van Gogh, in what might appear as a rare instance of bragging but was really just a stating of the facts, responded, "It is not really necessary. Later on they are bound to recognize my work, and they will surely write about me when I am dead. I will make sure of that if life grants me the time." When van Gogh did sign his name, however, he modestly only signed "Vincent."

Drawn as if by a magnet to that larger world of new art that Theo constantly told him about, van Gogh left Holland in November 1885. He would never return. He was then 32 years old and about to undergo one of the most striking stylistic transformations of any modern artist. He first stopped in Antwerp, Belgium, where he enrolled in art classes at the Antwerp Academy. Not surprisingly, he had

no patience with the academic style preached there. When the drawing master Eugeen Siberdt asked the students to sketch a plaster cast of the Venus de Milo, a well-known Greek sculpture, van Gogh drew a fleshy, wide-hipped figure, more a peasant woman than a classical goddess. When he saw the sketch, Siberdt had about the same reaction as van Rappard had to *The Potato Eaters,* and he tore up the sketch. Van Gogh flew into a rage, shouting that Siberdt had no idea what a woman was and that, as van Gogh reported to his brother later, she "must have hips, buttocks, a pelvis in which she can carry a baby."

Van Gogh was on to greater things than the Antwerp Academy could offer. In Antwerp, he had his first glimpse of the inexpensive Japanese prints then making their way into Europe. Van Gogh instantly took to the bold outlines, primary colors, subject matter, and simple, meditative look of Japanese woodcuts. In this indirect way, he began to get an idea of what Theo and, more to the point, the Impressionists meant by color. Van Gogh was now unstoppable. He quit the Antwerp Academy and in March 1886 abruptly left for Paris.

Van Gogh painted Le Moulin de la Galette *in the winter of 1886 while living in Paris. He frequented the cafés and streets of Montmartre, where Fernand Cormon's studio was located and where artists, entertainers, prostitutes, and working-class citizens resided. While studying with Cormon, van Gogh met artists Émile Bernard and Henri de Toulouse-Lautrec, both of whom would become his closest friends.*

6

A Singing Bird

ONE DAY IN MARCH 1886, Theo received a handwritten note in his office at Goupil's in Paris. It was from Vincent. Written crudely in black chalk, it said simply that he was in the Salle Carrée of the Louvre, France's foremost art museum, at that moment and hoped Theo could meet him there at once.

For Theo, Vincent's unexpected arrival in Paris came as a shock. Although Theo had been seeing to his brother's financial needs for years, it had always been from a distance. As he made his way to the Louvre, he must have wondered how his brother's sudden appearance would affect his own comfortable life. Unlike Vincent, Theo had stuck to the career on which Uncle Cent had started him and was now a distinguished art dealer. After more than a dozen years with Goupil's, he had become manager of one of the company's two Parisian branches and was authorized to buy and sell paintings at his own discretion.

Unbeknownst to Goupil's management, Theo became quite liberal in his interpretation of this mandate. He dealt in the standard academic paintings in which the company specialized, but his heart lay in the new painting styles. While the artwork of the old school hung prominently in the gallery, Theo secretly collected and stashed away a huge collection of works by Impressionist and Postimpressionist painters. After Theo's death, Goupil's top managers discovered this secret cache, mostly hidden away in the upstairs portion of the two-storied office. "Theo van Gogh has accumulated the most appalling stuff by modern painters," an angered Goupil's executive told Theo's replacement. "Just do the best you can with them and don't bother us, or we'll be obliged to close the place down." The "appalling stuff" included works by Edgar Degas, Paul Gauguin, Camille Pissarro, Odilon Redon, and Henri de Toulouse-Lautrec, among others—works that today grace the galleries of the world's leading art museums.

Theo van Gogh had one of the most discerning eyes for modern art in his day. The French poet Gustave Kahn described Theo as "pale, blond, and so melancholy that he seemed to hold canvases the way beggars hold their wooden bowls. His profound conviction of the value of the new art was stated without vigor, and thus without great success. He did not have a barker's gift. But this salesman was an excellent critic and engaged in discussions with painters and writers as the discriminating art lover he was."

Although Vincent's sudden arrival took him by surprise, Theo realized he could finally show his struggling artist-brother the new styles that he had for so long—and so futilely, it seemed—described in his letters. To accommodate the two of them, Theo rented a more spacious apartment in the Rue Lepic in the Montmartre section of Paris. The space, which the brothers moved into immediately, included a small studio for Vincent, who vigorously set to work. Theo wrote to their mother in Holland:

We are getting along well in the new flat; you would not
recognize Vincent, he has changed so much, and other
people find it even more striking than I do. . . . The doctor
says that he is now hale and hearty again. He is making
tremendous progress in his work and is beginning to
succeed. He is also far more cheerful than before, and is
very well liked. For example, he has some friends who
each week send him a nice consignment of flowers for him
to paint. He paints mainly flowers, above all in order to
freshen up his colors for future paintings. If we can keep
it up, then I think he has the worst behind him; and he is
going to come out on top.

With Theo's help, Vincent immersed himself in the avant-
garde art world of Paris. On the streets of Montmartre, he
met Camille Pissarro, the white-bearded patriarch who,
with Claude Monet, had pioneered Impressionism 15 years
before. Pissarro, a kind old man, patiently showed the
young artist his work and gave him advice about painting.
Van Gogh met other artists at an art supply store owned
by a former soldier affectionately called Père ("father")
Tanguy. Tanguy's cubbyhole shop had become a meeting
place for modern artists as well as an informal art gallery—
Tanguy often accepted artists' paintings as payment for art
materials. For a time, Tanguy's was the only place in Paris
where one could view works by Paul Cézanne, who would
eventually become one of the most influential painters in
modern art.

   Overwhelmed by the new styles, with their preternatu-
ral bright colors and lightness, van Gogh threw himself
into experiments. In order to improve his technical style,
he began soon after his arrival to study under a minor
academic painter named Fernand Cormon, who had made
a name for himself—short-lived, as it turned out—as a
painter of huge canvases of historical subjects (Greek
myths, nymphs, and landscapes) and portraits. Although
van Gogh characteristically quit Cormon's studio within
several weeks, there he met two modern painters who

Julien Tanguy, fondly called Père Tanguy, owned an artist supply shop in Montmartre and accepted many of the Impressionists' artworks in exchange for materials. Van Gogh painted this portrait of Tanguy in the winter of 1887 after Camille Pissarro persuaded him to abandon his dismal palette. In the background of the portrait, van Gogh included several of the Japanese prints he so eagerly collected.

would become two of his closest friends, Émile Bernard and Henri de Toulouse-Lautrec.

Eschewing for good the need to study under anyone, van Gogh instead began copying the new styles. He became friends with Paul Signac, who, with Georges Seurat, had pioneered the Neoimpressionist style called Pointillism. Pointillists stippled their canvases with points, or dots, of pure color, which, when viewed from a few feet away, "mixed" in the viewer's eye to create lovely, soft scenes and produce intense color effects. The most renowned painting to come out of this short-lived but influential style was Seurat's massive work *Sunday Afternoon on the Island of La Grande Jatte* (1884–86). Van Gogh's own

Interior of a Restaurant (1887) shows this stippling style in the walls and floor (though the brushstroke-painted chairs and picture frames reveal his attachment to the standard Impressionist style of painting). Another example of the Impressionists' influence on van Gogh's technique can be seen in his painting *Fritillaries* (see page 65), especially in the speckled background. On the banks of the Seine, van Gogh worked alongside Signac, who was a native of Montmartre. "Van Gogh, wearing the blue overalls of a zinc worker, would have little dots of color painted on his shirt sleeves," Signac later recalled. "Sticking quite close to me, he would be yelling, gesticulating, and brandishing a large, size thirty, freshly painted canvas; in this fashion he would manage to polychrome both himself and the passers-by."

Van Gogh also became smitten with the style of the Japanese masters. Beginning in the late 18th and early 19th centuries, artists such as Katsushika Hokusai and Ando Hiroshige had begun to master a form of art known as *ukiyo-e* ("pictures of the floating world"). To the Japanese, this floating world had two meanings: first, in the traditional sense, it meant a transient, imaginary place; and second, in a contemporary sense, it referred to the sensual age in which the art was being developed—in other words, the "modern" world of the flesh, focusing on the realms of the theater and the brothel. Ukiyo-e artists used woodblock printing, or woodcutting, in which color prints are made from designs cut in relief on wood, to create striking landscapes, portraits, and other works. As subjects, these Japanese artists focused on beautiful courtesans, Kabuki theater actors, and landscapes in which they depicted common people performing everyday tasks. It was only after Commodore Matthew Perry "opened" Japan to Western goods and tourists on his historic voyage of 1853 that Japanese prints first began to be seen outside of the Asian country. Soon, however, inexpensive prints could be had in European cities, including Paris, which featured Japanese prints at its world art exhibitions of 1867 and 1878 and in a solo show in 1883. Interestingly, these Japanese artists were originally influenced by Dutch engravers whose prints made their way to Japan via various shipping routes. Perhaps it is no surprise, then, that the Dutchman van Gogh—not to mention many other contemporary artists in Europe—became so enamored of such works as Hokusai's *Thirty-six Views of Mount Fuji* (circa 1823–33) and Hiroshige's landscape series, *Fifty-three Stations of the Tokaido Highway* (1833).

Van Gogh amassed a collection of Japanese prints, which he bought for a few francs each in the streets of Montmartre, and began imitating the ukiyo-e style in his oil paintings. His *Japonaiserie: Trees in Bloom* of 1887 shows a striking change from his former work, with bright primary colors (red, blue, and yellow), bold outlines, and a flattened perspective as well as a border of Japanese calligraphy. Indeed, the painting's garden scene, with dark, twisted trees in the foreground and small, dehumanized people in the distance, eerily foreshadows paintings of the garden at Saint-Rémy, the hospital he entered not long after his mental breakdown in December 1888.

Although van Gogh did many exercises in Pointillism and the style of the ukiyo-e masters, he was most taken with Impressionism and made numerous studies in that style. In the two years he lived in Paris, van Gogh produced about 200 paintings, including some 35 still lifes and about 50 each of flowers and landscapes—a prodigious output by any standard. Most of these paintings reveal the utter transformation he underwent after coming into contact with Impressionism, changing from a self-described "shaggy dog" painter in his dark-toned Holland years to what one art critic called a "singing bird" in his final years in France.

A Woman in the Café Le Tambourin of 1887, an attempt at a traditional Impressionist scene (a woman sitting alone in a café), strongly blends elements of both the somber style he was shedding and the lively style he was assuming. The still-heavy dose of browns and bland yellows and especially the blocky, rough-hewn figure and face of the woman hark back to such earlier works as *The Potato Eaters*. But here, too, is color quite unlike what he had ever used before, done in the short, slashing brushstrokes so characteristic of the Impressionists. Behind the woman is a grass-green wall displaying, not coincidentally, a brightly colored Japanese print, while the edge of the table she is sitting at is bright red, a color echoed in the material of her tall hat. Soon van Gogh would dispense with the browns and somber yellows for a palette solely made up of the most vivid primary colors.

Van Gogh painted the impressionistic A Woman in the Café Le Tambourin *in the beginning of 1887. Le Tambourin, which got its name from its tabletops that were made to look like tambourines, was owned by Agostina Segatori, allegedly the woman seen here and with whom van Gogh had an affair.*

The painting *A Woman in the Café Le Tambourin* says
as much in content as in style about van Gogh's life at this
time. Le Tambourin was frequented by many avant-garde
artists and soon became van Gogh's favorite watering
place. Here he came to talk art with his friends Émile
Bernard and Henri de Toulouse-Lautrec, who painted a
portrait of van Gogh in the café drinking a glass of absinthe. (Until it was banned as harmful in 1915, absinthe,
a green-colored, licorice-tasting drink originally marketed
as a health cordial, was a highly fashionable alcoholic
beverage.) The woman depicted in the painting is believed
to be Agostina Segatori, the Italian woman who owned Le
Tambourin and who for a short period might have been van
Gogh's mistress. And the Japanese prints on the wall are
likely van Gogh's, for he had convinced La Segatori, as
she was known, to let him hang a selection from his
collection, which went up in March 1887. She even allowed him to put up his own work, which soon covered the
walls. But sometime in the spring La Segatori had a
falling-out with van Gogh over a fight he had had with one
of her employees or customers (it is not clear which), and
he was never able to retrieve his paintings. Tragically, in
the years following, La Segatori apparently sold the paintings as waste canvas in bundles of 10, for as little as 10
cents per bundle.

Although the details of van Gogh's fight at Le Tambourin will probably never be known, the incident was
indicative of his increasingly unstable nature. He had
begun to drink heavily, mostly the highly addictive absinthe, which only exacerbated his peculiar tendencies.
Archibald Hartrick, a British painter who befriended van
Gogh in Paris, remembered him as "a rather weedy little
man, with pinched features, red hair and beard, and light
blue eyes. He had an extraordinary way of pouring out
sentences, if he got started, in Dutch, English, and French,
then glancing back at you over his shoulder and hissing
through his teeth. In fact, when thus excited, he looked

more than a little mad; at other times he was apt to be morose, as if suspicious." Hartrick drew a telling sketch of van Gogh that seems to capture that very habit. Other artists also remarked on his beginning madness. Not long after van Gogh's death, his friend and mentor Camille Pissarro is reported to have said that he was sure that van Gogh "would either go mad or leave all of us far behind. I didn't know then that he would do both." And Paul Cézanne, upon meeting van Gogh in Père Tanguy's art supply shop, supposedly told him, "Sir, you paint like a madman."

Even Theo was at his wit's end with his brother. He poured out his heart to his sister Wilhelmina in Holland:

> My home life is almost unbearable; no one wants to come to see me any more because it always ends in quarrels; besides, he is so untidy that the place looks far from attractive. I wish he would go and live by himself; he sometimes speaks about it, but if I were to tell him to go away, it would be just a reason for him to stay. Since I can do nothing right for him, I only ask for one thing: that he does not cause me any trouble. But by staying with me he is doing just that, for I can hardly bear it.

Theo went on to describe his brother's split personality, not the last reference to a possible schizophrenia (a mental disorder in which a person loses touch with reality; it is characterized by profound emotional withdrawal and bizarre behavior, and often includes delusions and hallucinations). "It is as if he had two persons in him—one marvelously gifted, delicate and tender, the other egotistical and hardhearted," he wrote to his sister. "They present themselves in turn, so that one hears him talk first in one way, then in the other, and this always with arguments which are now all for, now all against the same point. It is a pity that he is his own enemy, for he makes life hard not only for others but for himself." When Wilhelmina advised him to "leave Vincent for God's sake," Theo answered with his characteristic thoughtfulness, which reveals yet

again his unshakable loyalty to his older brother. "It is
such a peculiar case," he wrote. "If he only had another
profession, I would long ago have done what you advise
me. I have often asked myself if I have not been wrong in
helping him continually, and have often been on the point
of leaving him to his own devices . . . but I think in this
case I must continue in the same way. He is certainly an
artist, and if what he makes now is not always beautiful,
cit will certainly be of use to him later; then his work will
perhaps be sublime."

In the end, Theo did not have to make the hard decision
to leave his brother, for Vincent abruptly left Paris on
February 20, 1888, for the south of France. It is not known
for certain why van Gogh departed, but some people believe it was because he was jealous of his brother's increas-
ing affection for a young woman named Johanna Bonger.
During the previous summer, Vincent, in an odd reference
to the courtship, had written to Theo, then vacationing in
Holland, that "it's better to have a gay life of it than commit
suicide." (He added, "As for me—I feel I am losing the
desire for marriage and children, and now and then it
saddens me that I should be feeling like that at thirty-five,
just when it should be the opposite.") He had also begun
to feel overwhelmed by the intensity of the Parisian art
world and stifled by the unspoken competition between
painters. "I will take myself off somewhere down south,"
he declared in that same letter, "to get away from the sight
of so many painters that disgust me as men." He had begun
arguing constantly with other artists, to the point where
even friends such as Archibald Hartrick thought him a bit
"cracked." (Van Gogh himself admitted that "I cannot
always keep quiet.") The final blow came early in the year
when Paul Gauguin, one of his closest friends in Paris,
moved to Brittany on the northwestern French coast.

Nor does anyone know why van Gogh was so powerfully drawn to the Midi, the south of France. His friend
Henri de Toulouse-Lautrec, a native of Languedoc, had

In this self-portrait of 1887, van Gogh's short and disjointed brushstrokes appear to be elongated versions of Pointillistic dots. Artist Paul Cézanne once remarked to van Gogh, "Sir, you paint like a madman."

long raved to him about the nearby region of Provence, and Paul Signac had moved there the previous summer. Incongruously, van Gogh came to think of the Midi (which he had never visited) as the European equivalent of the Japanese landscape (which he had never seen). Unable to resist the pull of his dream landscape any longer, van Gogh suddenly announced to Theo in February that he was leaving, planning to travel first to Arles and then on to the port city of Marseilles on the Mediterranean Sea.

Van Gogh's Self-Portrait, *painted in the fall of 1889, represents a return to figure painting for the artist, who had only painted landscapes from May to July. Corresponding with Theo, he remarked, "They say—and I am very willing to believe it—that it is difficult to know yourself—but it isn't easy to paint yourself either."*

7

"A TERRIBLE AND MADDENED GENIUS"

FOR VAN GOGH, Arles came as a revelation. A small agricultural town on the Rhône River about 55 miles from the Mediterranean, Arles lies in the heart of the Midi. The Midi is a region of soft light and pleasant climate that has lured visitors ever since the Roman rulers Julius Caesar and Constantine the Great sojourned there, leaving behind aqueducts, theaters, and tombs that even today lend the town a classical air.

But van Gogh was not interested in Roman artifacts. For him, Arles offered a visual feast of rural scenes, brilliant color, and soft, ever-changing light. Soon after arriving, van Gogh ecstatically described to Theo "a meadow full of very yellow buttercups, a ditch with irises, green leaves and purple flowers, the town in the background, some gray willows, and a strip of blue sky." The "color, color, color" he had

91

mused on all day on that visit to the Rijksmuseum in Amsterdam in 1885 had finally taken hold with a vengeance. He assured Theo that "the painter of the future will be a colorist such as has never existed."

He had no idea how right he was. Van Gogh was then in the process of becoming the most intense colorist of his day, and along with other Postimpressionists such as Paul Cézanne, he was setting the stage for future movements based solely on color, such as Abstract Expressionism in the years following World War II. Though few realized it at the time, painters like van Gogh heralded the end of representation, in which artists depicted recognizable objects or scenes, and the beginning of abstraction, in which they used shapes, lines, textures, and, above all, color to spark thoughts and emotions in the beholder.

Van Gogh's letters at this time reveal almost joyously how, after years of toil, he had finally hit his stride as an artist. There is an intensity and a sureness of purpose heretofore unknown in his writings. In a letter to Theo shortly after his arrival in Arles, van Gogh confidently described the manner and meaning of his painting.

> I hit the canvas with irregular touches of the brush, which I leave as they are. Patches of thickly laid-on color, spots of canvas left uncovered, here and there with portions that are left absolutely unfinished, repetitions, savageries. . . . Working directly on the spot all the time, I try to grasp what is essential in the drawing—later I fill in the spaces that are bounded by contours—either expressed or not, but in any case *felt*—with tones that are also simplified, by which I mean that all that is going to be soil will share the same violet-like tone, that the whole sky will have a blue tint.

In these lines, van Gogh succinctly reveals how and why he works. He always worked directly from nature, often sitting all day long in the same spot. *The Bridge at Langlois* (see page 67), executed in March 1888, is considered by many art historians to be one of the most successful paintings of the Arles period. He also frequently visited the Mediterranean town of Saintes-Maries-de-la-Mer, to which Gypsies from around the world would annually come to celebrate a religious festival. Van Gogh painted *Gypsy Camp* (see page 66) during one such visit in August 1888. He was, as he put it, "a painting engine," who cheated darkness by sticking lighted candles in the brim of his hat and heading out into the night to paint. "Today again from seven o'clock in the morning till six in the evening I worked without stirring except to take some food a step or two away," he told Theo. "I have no thought of fatigue, I shall do another picture this very night, and I shall bring it off." Later, while under the care of Dr. Felix Rey at the Arles hospital, he admitted to Theo that "M. Rey says that instead of eating enough and at regular times, I kept myself going on coffee and alcohol. I admit all that, but all the same it is true that to attain the high yellow note I attained last summer, I really had to be pretty well keyed up."

That "high yellow note," captured so enduringly in the *Sunflower* paintings he executed that summer and fall, represented to van Gogh both color and emotion. In van Gogh's *Still-Life, Vase with Fourteen Sunflowers* (August 1888), for example, it seems as though the artist painted each stem and flower with a spectacular vitality so that natural energy is conveyed through the individual blossoms rather than through the collective whole of the bouquet. In order to express the "sincere human feeling" van Gogh had described to Theo, he strove in his work "to exaggerate the essential, and purposely leave the obvious things vague." In a poetic passage from a letter to Theo in August 1888, he passionately detailed his modus operandi (method of working):

> I should like to paint the portrait of an artist friend, a man who dreams great dreams, who works as the nightingale sings, because it is his nature. He'll be a blond man. I want

to put my appreciation, the love I have for him, into the picture. So I paint him as he is, as faithfully as I can, to begin with. . . . But the picture is not yet finished. To finish it I am now going to be the arbitrary colorist. I exaggerate the fairness of the hair, I even get to orange tones, chromes and pale citron-yellow. . . . Behind the head, instead of painting the ordinary wall of the mean room, I paint infinity, a plain background of the richest, most intense blue I can contrive, and by this simple combination of the bright head against the rich blue background I get a mysterious effect, like a star in the depths of an azure sky.

In another portrait, that of a peasant working the harvest under the blazing Midi sun, van Gogh goes for a different effect using the same technique: "I imagine the man I have to paint, tormented in the furnace heat at the height of the harvest time, as surrounded by the whole Midi. Hence the orange colors flashing like lightning, vivid as a red-hot iron, and hence the luminous tones of old gold in the shadows. Oh, my dear boy," he added, "and the good people will only see the exaggeration as caricature."

Like all true visionaries, van Gogh expected not to be understood right away. His color scheme was radical even by Impressionist standards, and the sheer quantity of the works he turned out—some 100 paintings and 90 drawings from his arrival in Arles in February to his debilitating attack in December—would appear to some, he knew, to preclude quality. But he warned Theo against this. "Quick work doesn't mean less serious work, it depends on one's self-confidence and experience. In the same way Jules Guérard, the lion hunter, says in his book that in the beginning young lions have a lot of trouble killing a horse or an ox, but that old lions kill with a single blow of the paw or a well-placed bite, and that they are amazingly sure at the job." In a subsequent letter, he wrote on the same subject. "Is it not emotion, the sincerity of one's feeling for nature, that drives us? And if the emotions are sometimes so strong that one works without knowing one works, when sometimes the strokes come with a continuity and a coherence like words in a speech or a letter, then one must remember that it has not always been so, and that in times to come there will be hard days, empty of inspiration. So one must strike while the iron is hot, and put the forged bars on one side." Indeed, van Gogh's productivity came to an abrupt halt on December 23, 1888, the night he had a severe mental breakdown and slashed his own ear.

If he expected not to be understood by the critics, he expected even less from the people of Arles. In the 15 months he lived in Arles, van Gogh made but two friends: the town postman, Joseph Roulin, whose portrait (see page 69) and the portraits of other members of Roulin's family he painted many times, and Paul-Eugène Milliet, a French lieutenant on leave in Arles. A member of the Zouaves, a regiment of light infantry then stationed at Arles, Milliet was, compared to the Arlesian peasants, a cultured man who enjoyed sketching and discussing art. Milliet understood van Gogh as the provincial people of Arles could not:

> He was a charming companion when he knew what he wanted—which didn't happen every day. We often went on good walks around Arles, and in the country we would make no end of sketches. Sometimes he would set up his canvas and start daubing straight away. After that there was no budging him. The fellow had talent in his drawing, but he became quite different when he picked up his brushes. As soon as he started painting I would leave him alone, otherwise I should have to refuse to tell him what I thought, or we would start arguing. He hadn't got an easy nature and when he lost his temper you'd think he'd gone mad.

Notwithstanding Roulin and Milliet, van Gogh, even though he lived like a peasant himself, felt far removed spiritually and intellectually from the townspeople of Arles. "Must I tell the truth," he confessed to Theo, "and add that the Zouaves, the brothels, the adorable little

Arlésiennes going to their first Communion, the priest in his surplice, who looks like a dangerous rhinoceros, the people drinking absinthe, all seem to me like creatures from another world."

The feeling was mutual. Not without reason, the people of Arles took issue with van Gogh's habits, which became increasingly slovenly and peculiar as his first year in Arles progressed. (Even Paul Gauguin, who arrived in October, felt van Gogh's personal habits and hygiene a bit shocking.) Children taunted him, adults avoided him. Soon after his mental breakdown in December, local youths began throwing rocks at the windows of the Yellow House to intimidate him. Distraught and angered, van Gogh took to screaming back at them. This prompted 30 residents to sign a petition in January 1889 to the mayor requesting that van Gogh be locked up. One day in early February, their wish was granted: the police arrived at the Yellow House and hauled van Gogh off again to the hospital, where he was locked in a cell for dangerous lunatics. "What a staggering blow between the eyes it was," he told Theo, "to find so many people here cowardly enough to join together against one man, and that man ill."

Van Gogh remained at the Arles hospital for several months. Initially, he was not allowed to paint, but before long he was moved out of solitary confinement and into a room where he was provided again with his paints and brushes. He assured Theo that he was "in full possession of my faculties, not a madman but the brother you know." Painting became his only means of escaping a deepening depression he felt in the Arles hospital, as well as a way of getting back at the injustices he felt had been visited upon him by the people of Arles. "The more ugly, old, vicious, ill, poor I get," he confessed to Theo, "the more I want to take my revenge by producing a brilliant color, well-arranged, resplendent." On March 23, he was granted permission to take a walk with Paul Signac, who had come to visit him. The two went to the Yellow House, where van

Gogh showed his friend his paintings. "All day long he talked about painting, literature, socialism," Signac recalled. "In the evening he was a little tired. There was a terrific mistral [a cold, violent wind of the region that is believed to cause strange behavior] blowing which may have unnerved him. He wanted to drink a liter of turpentine directly out of the container which was on the table of the bedroom. It was time for him to return to the hospital."

But the Arles hospital was woefully ill-equipped to care for a mentally unstable patient, and van Gogh continued to suffer from "a certain undercurrent of vague sadness difficult to define." When a local pastor told him

In The Hospital in Arles *of April 1889, van Gogh depicted one of the hospital wards in which he recuperated after his breakdown. He wrote to his sister Wilhelmina, "I have had in all four great crises during which I didn't in the least know what I said, what I wanted and what I did."*

of Saint Paul's, a mental hospital in the nearby town of Saint-Rémy, where he might get better care, van Gogh immediately wrote to the director, Dr. Théophile Peyron, requesting permission to be admitted there. Theo, as always, lent a hand as well. "In view of the fact that his internment is desired mainly to prevent the recurrence

Van Gogh painted this view of the asylum garden at Saint-Rémy in November 1889. The brushstrokes of the pine tree convey profound energy; van Gogh, who struggled with recurring spells of madness and intense creativity while at the asylum, painted several canvases of its garden and majestic trees. Some scholars believe the painting's hatted figure standing in the doorway is a self-portrait.

of previous attacks and not because his mental condition is unsound," Theo wrote to Peyron, "I hope that you will find it possible to permit him to do some painting outside of your establishment. . . . I beg you to be kind enough to allow him at least a half liter of wine with his meals."

Peyron accepted the terms and admitted van Gogh on May 8, 1889. Called Saint Paul-de-Mausole, the hospital was colloquially known as the Asylum for the Alienated. Originally an Augustinian monastery dating to the 13th century, it became a mental hospital run by Catholic nuns in the early 1800s and is still in use today. It consists of two long dormitories, one for women, one for men, containing spartan cells with bars on the windows. Outside is a walled garden with trees, a fountain, and a few benches; in the distance lie the Alpilles, a ridge of limestone hills. Here, in a tiny room on the second floor "with greenish-gray paper and two curtains of sea-green with a design of very pale roses, brightened by slight touches of blood red," van Gogh would spend the next year of his life, alternating between bouts of madness and fierce creativity.

The exact nature of his illness was, and still is, unknown. Upon van Gogh's admittance, Peyron wrote that he "is suffering from acute mania with hallucinations of sight and hearing which have caused him to mutilate himself by cutting off his ear. At present he seems to have recovered his reason, but he does not feel that he possesses the strength and the courage to live independently . . . my opinion is that M. van Gogh is subject to epileptic fits at very infrequent intervals." (Epilepsy is defined as any of various nervous disorders associated with abnormal electrical activity in an injured portion of the brain and typically takes the form of convulsive seizures.) Van Gogh's attacks came on while painting outdoors or on the few occasions when he was allowed away from the hospital. But van Gogh did not seem to have suffered the convulsive seizures that characterize epileptic fits, which has led some physicians to dismiss epilepsy as a possible affliction.

Many diagnoses, including paranoid schizophrenia (a mental disorder characterized by anxiety, anger, violent behavior, and delusions of persecution or grandeur), manic depression (a mental disorder in which a person's mood alternates between very high—mania—and very low—depression), acute intermittent porphyria (a metabolic disorder), and a brain damaged by alcoholism or syphilis (a contagious venereal disease), have been made in the decades since van Gogh's death.

Although no one, then or now, could give a definitive clinical name to his malady, van Gogh described it in his distinctively vivid detail in letters to Theo. Perhaps the most tragic aspect of van Gogh's illness was that it isolated this already unnaturally removed man even further. "When you suffer much," he confided in Theo, "you see everybody at a great distance, and as at the far end of a room or an immense arena—the very voices seem to come from afar. During the attacks I experience this to such a degree that all the persons I see then, even if I recognize them, which is not always the case, seem to come toward me out of a great distance, and to be quite different from what they are in reality." For van Gogh, however, the worst part was not the feeling of being utterly alone but the fear and horror of the attacks, which came on suddenly and would last for days or weeks at a time.

Despite being subjected to the "terrible howls and cries like those of beasts in a menagerie" erupting day and night from other rooms, van Gogh ironically found comfort in being among people who suffered, as he did, inexplicable and utterly debilitating attacks. "I gather from others," he wrote to Theo, "that during their attacks they have also heard strange sounds and voices as I did, and that in their eyes too things seemed to be changing. And that lessens the horror that I retained at first of the attack I have had, and which, when it comes on you unawares, cannot but frighten you beyond measure. Once you know that it is part of the disease, you take it like anything else. If I had not seen other lunatics close up, I should not have been able to free myself from dwelling on it constantly."

Except when attacks came on, van Gogh was largely free to do as he wished. Peyron prescribed hydrotherapy: two-hour soakings in a tub of water twice a week. Other than that, van Gogh received no regular treatment, and was more like a boarder in a hotel—a cheap hotel, where the food, he complained to Theo, "tastes rather moldy, as in a cockroach-infested restaurant in Paris or in a boarding-house." He was given a second room as a studio, and whenever his condition allowed it, he painted at his usual frantic pace. Within a few weeks of his arrival at Saint-Rémy, Peyron allowed him to walk abroad with an attendant in the cultivated fields nearby in order to paint.

He became enamored of the cypress trees that rose like black flames from the earth. The trees "are always occupying my thoughts," he confided to his brother. "I should like to make something of them like the canvases of the sunflowers, because it astonishes me that they have not yet been done as I see them. The tree is as beautiful of line and proportion as an Egyptian obelisk. And the green has a quality of such distinction. It is a splash of black in a sunny landscape, but it is one of the most interesting black notes, and the most difficult to hit off exactly that I can imagine." In the end, van Gogh's undulating, vibrantly alive paintings and drawings of cypresses, such as those prominently displayed in *The Starry Night* (see page 72), have become as much a symbol of his intense personality as the sunflowers he so loved.

In July 1889 Peyron granted him permission to travel, with a hospital guard, to his house in Arles to get some canvases. He had been healthy for some months, had been painting nonstop, and had been reading Shakespeare's history plays, which Theo had sent him. Theo had now been married for four months to Johanna, who announced in a letter to her brother-in-law that, sometime in the winter, the couple would have a baby, "whom we are going to call Vincent, if you will kindly consent to be his god-father."

The news and the trip to Arles proved too much for van Gogh. Soon after his return to the hospital, he tried to kill himself by eating his paints, which he squeezed from their tubes like toothpaste. Peyron confined him for his own protection and closed his studio. It was several weeks before he returned to his senses, and many more before he was up and around. "It is splendid weather outside, but for a long time—two months to be exact—I have not left my room," Vincent wrote to his sister Wilhelmina. "I don't know why. What I need is courage, and this often fails me. And it is also a fact that since my disease, when I am in the fields I am overcome by a feeling of loneliness to such a horrible extent that I shy away from going out. . . . Only when I stand painting before my easel do I feel somewhat alive." Though Peyron had unlocked his studio, he re-mained in his room, copying prints after Delacroix, Millet, and Rembrandt that Theo had mailed to him.

The pain and horror of the attacks made van Gogh contemplate suicide. "Every day I take the remedy which the incomparable [novelist Charles] Dickens prescribes against suicide," he confided to Theo. "It consists of a glass of wine, a piece of bread with cheese and a pipe of tobacco. This is not complicated, you will tell me, and you will hardly be able to believe that this is the limit to which melancholy will take me; all the same, at some moments— oh, dear me." On the whole he was like someone swim-ming upstream, always on the verge of being swept away by the current. "Well, it is not always pleasant," he contin-ued, "but I do my best not to forget altogether how to make contemptuous fun of it. I try to avoid anything that has any connection with heroism or martyrdom; in short, I do my best not to take lugubrious things lugubriously." Work, as always, proved his salvation:

> Life passes like this, time does not return, but I am dead
> set on my work, for just this very reason, that I know the

opportunities of working do not return. Especially in my case, in which a more violent attack may forever destroy my power to paint. . . . During the attacks I feel cowardly toward the pain and suffering—more of a coward than I ought to be, and it is perhaps this very moral cowardice which, whereas I had no desire to get better before, makes me eat like two now, work hard, limit my relations with the other patients for fear of a relapse—altogether I am now trying to recover like a man who meant to commit suicide and, finding the water too cold, tries to regain the bank.

The attacks continued. On December 23, 1889, a year to the day after his first fit in Arles, he suffered another. Again he ate paint, and he even tried to guzzle a container full of kerosene; attendants forced the poisons up. Again Peyron refused to let him paint, feeling that his work triggered the lapses. And again he recovered rapidly, appeared perfectly sane, and was allowed to resume work. The routine had become sickeningly familiar.

Then, in early 1890, three events occurred that should have considerably bucked up van Gogh's spirits. First, he became an uncle. On January 31, Johanna gave birth to a boy, who, as promised the summer before, became his namesake, Vincent Willem van Gogh. Because he could not see his new nephew right away, van Gogh set to work immediately on a gift for little Vincent, an almost tapestry-like painting of white-blossomed almond branches against a bright blue sky.

About the same time, Theo informed him that an article about his work had appeared in the avant-garde magazine *Le Mercure de France.* Aptly titled "Les Isolés" (The isolated ones), the piece was written by a young critic named G.-Albert Aurier and was highly favorable of van Gogh's work:

What particularly characterizes all these works is the excess, excess in strength, excess in nervousness, in violence of expression . . . in his frequently headstrong simplification of forms, in his insolence in depicting the sun face to face . . . he reveals a powerful being, a male, a bold man, often brutal and sometimes ingenuously delicate . . . a kind of drunken giant, better able to move mountains than to handle *bibelots* [knickknacks], an ebullient brain which irresistibly pours its lava into all the ravines of art, a terrible and maddened genius, often sublime, sometimes grotesque, almost always on the edge of the pathological. . . . His color is unbelievably dazzling. He is, as far as I know, the only painter who perceives the coloration of things with such intensity.

Although the praise served as corroboration of Theo's blind faith in him, van Gogh felt the article was too flattering. He wrote Aurier a long letter on February 11, thanking him for the piece and telling him that "I rediscover my canvases in your article." But he went on at length to downplay his position in the pantheon of painters, telling Aurier that "the part which is allotted to me, or will be allotted to me, will remain, I assure you, very secondary."

Finally, van Gogh learned that one of his paintings had been sold at a show in Brussels. The show was put on by a group of artists and writers known as Les Vingt (The Twenty), which annually exhibited what it considered to be the finest modern paintings. Upon request from the 1890 exhibition's curator, Theo sent six of his brother's works. (A Les Vingt member, a Belgian painter of religious scenes named Henri de Groux, adamantly refused to have his paintings hung beside "the abominable *Pot of Sunflowers*," one of the paintings Theo had sent. Though de Groux had never met van Gogh, he denounced him to other Les Vingt members as "an ignoramus and a charlatan." Unluckily for de Groux, one of those members happened to be Henri de Toulouse-Lautrec, who immediately challenged him to a duel. While other Les Vingt members put a stop to the duel, de Groux was forced to resign the next day.) One of van Gogh's paintings at the show was *The Red Vineyards,* which a Belgian artist

named Anna Boch bought for 400 Belgian francs (about $80). It was the only one of van Gogh's paintings sold during his lifetime.

But for van Gogh, the news of the baby, the article, and the sale were overshadowed by his illness. On February 22, while putting the finishing touches on the gift painting for his nephew, van Gogh succumbed again. This time it took a full two months to recover. "My work was going well," he told Theo, "the last canvas of branches in blos-

Belgian artist Anna Boch bought van Gogh's The Red Vineyards *(1888), his only work to be sold during his lifetime, when she saw it exhibited at the 1890 Les Vingt show in Brussels.*

som—you will see that it was perhaps the best, the most patiently worked thing I had done, painted with calm and a greater firmness of touch. And the next day, down like a brute. Difficult to understand, things like that, but alas!"

In April, after he had recovered from the attack, he wrote of the sale and the article in a postscript to a letter to his mother and sister in Holland: "As soon as I heard that my work was having some success, and read the article in question, I feared at once that I should be punished for it; this is how things nearly always go in a painter's life: success is about the worst thing that can happen." He does not elaborate on why he felt this way. Perhaps his seesaw condition—now lucid and creative, now insane and listless—left him with the certainty that, despite his earlier belief in the unflinching optimism of *Candide*'s Father Pangloss, any good must be tempered with bad.

Because his condition did not seem to be improving—and Peyron gave him little hope to think otherwise—van Gogh began in early 1890 to contemplate leaving Saint-Rémy. He had begun suffering from religious hallucinations sparked, he feared, by his constant contact with the hospital's zealous Catholic nuns. As a comfort in his loneliness and despair, he thought often of his childhood home in Holland. "During my illness," he wrote, "I saw again every room in the house at Zundert, every path, every plant in the garden, the view of the fields outside, the neighbors, the graveyard, the church, our kitchen garden at the back—down to a magpie's nest in a tall acacia in the graveyard." The February attack left him all but incapacitated for two months. Unlike his former productivity even while recovering, the only work he managed to produce during that time was a series of drawings called *Memories of the North*. The tiny sketches, including a thatched cottage and a couple in a carriage, revert to his first hesitant sketches as an artist. His despair had reached its nadir, and he felt his only hope of recovery lay in his homeland, in being near his family. On April 24, as he came out of his stupor, he wrote to Theo:

> I take up this letter again to try to write, it will come little by little, the thing is that my head is so bad, without pain it is true, but altogether stupefied. I must tell you that there are, as far as I can judge, others who have the same thing wrong with them that I have, and who, after having worked part of their life, are reduced to helplessness now. It isn't easy to learn much good between four walls, that's natural, but all the same it is true that there are people who can no longer be left at liberty as though there were nothing wrong with them. And that means that I am pretty well or altogether in despair about myself. Perhaps I might really recover if I were in the country for a time.

Van Gogh asked his brother if he might approach Camille Pissarro, the fatherly Impressionist painter whom he had befriended in Paris, about allowing van Gogh to come work with him. Pissarro was all for it, but his wife felt that van Gogh might be a poor influence on their children. As a compromise, Pissarro suggested his young friend look up a certain Dr. Paul-Ferdinand Gachet in Auvers-sur-Oise, a village near Paris. Gachet had put up other painters who wished to work in the countryside, and he might be able to help van Gogh.

In May, van Gogh finally felt well enough to travel. On May 16, he boarded a train bound for Paris.

Van Gogh painted Dr. Gachet's Garden *in Auvers in May 1890. The artist wrote to Theo about the plants that he saw in the garden, identifying them as aloes, cypresses, and marigolds. Van Gogh gave each plant in the painting a mystical quality, magnifying individual details.*

8

A BOLD
FORWARD THRUST

FOR VAN GOGH, it was as if he had been released from prison. Theo met him at the train station in Paris and brought him home to meet his wife and baby. Johanna was surprised to find that her brother-in-law seemed, at least on the surface, healthier than her husband, who suffered from a chronic kidney ailment only exacerbated by heated arguments with his employers. "I had expected a sick man," she recalled later, "but here was a sturdy, broad-shouldered man with a healthy color, a smile on his face and a very resolute appearance."

The three days van Gogh spent at Theo's were filled with the flush of familial love. So long starved for affection, van Gogh absorbed the attentions of his brother and sister-in-law like a sponge. He was in unusually good spirits. "The first morning he was up very early and was standing in his shirtsleeves looking at his pictures, of which our apartment was full," Johanna remembered later. Some of van Gogh's greatest masterpieces graced the humble walls of Theo's apartment: in the dining room, *The Potato Eaters;* in the sitting room, the *Land-*

Van Gogh's sister-in-law Johanna Gesina van Gogh-Bonger poses with her son, Vincent Willem, in 1890. When van Gogh first saw his namesake during his visit to Paris in mid-May 1890, he told Johanna, "Don't cover him with too much lace, little sister."

scape of Arles and the *Night View on the Rhône*. Unframed canvases lay rolled up in every conceivable space, and "they were now spread out on the floor and studied with great attention," Johanna recalled. The most poignant moment came when Theo led his brother to the cradle of little Vincent. "Silently the two brothers looked at the quietly sleeping baby—both had tears in their eyes," Johanna recollected. "Then Vincent turned smilingly to me and said, pointing to the simple crocheted cover on the cradle, 'Don't cover him with too much lace, little sister.'"

Charged with newfound inspiration, van Gogh thought at first of remaining in Paris for a time to paint. Although any mention of Saint-Rémy and his illness were studiously avoided by all at Theo's, van Gogh's condition remained highly unstable. Van Gogh told Theo that he could not stand the noisy city and "[the noise] had such a bad effect on me that I thought it wise for my head's sake to fly to the country."

Within three days of arriving in the French capital, he began to feel the old agitation that, two years before, had forced him to leave Paris for the tranquillity of the south. He decided to depart immediately for Auvers-sur-Oise, the hamlet a half hour's journey north of Paris that Pissarro had recommended.

Auvers was ideal for a nervous soul like van Gogh. Much the same today as it was when he arrived in May 1890, Auvers is a sleepy agricultural village perched on the edge of the slow-moving Oise River. A group of thatched-roof houses on a slope above the river gives way, higher up, to acres and acres of trim farm fields. Van Gogh found Auvers "profoundly beautiful . . . the real country, characteristic and picturesque." So did a number of other painters who lived here for a time, including Pissarro, Cézanne, and Charles-François Daubigny, whom van Gogh greatly admired. Daubigny, primarily known for his poetic landscapes, had moved to Auvers in 1861. Van Gogh painted *Daubigny's Garden* (see pages 70 and 71) directly from nature.

In stark contrast to the soothing landscape of Auvers, however, was the room van Gogh rented at a local inn. Van Gogh considered it a steal at three francs fifty (about $ .70) per day with board. But the room was dark and cramped, with barely enough room for a bed, table, and chest of drawers. Like other apartments he had taken, it was situated up under the eaves, where a single clouded window and a tiny skylight let in but a fraction of the light that flooded the surrounding countryside. The inn survives to this day as the Auberge Ravoux, and its owners have carefully preserved the tiny third-floor room in which the artist died.

Van Gogh felt proud to have found cheaper lodgings than those recommended by the man whom Pissarro had

Dr. Paul-Ferdinand Gachet, a friend and patron of numerous artists, including Cézanne, Pissarro (who had recommended him to van Gogh), Monet, and Renoir, among others, was an eccentric man according to van Gogh. He told Theo that Dr. Gachet was "as ill and distraught as you or me," and he painted this portrait of Dr. Gachet "with the heartbroken expression of our time."

sent him to see. Dr. Paul Gachet was a 61-year-old wid-
ower who proved van Gogh's equal in oddness. Red-
haired, with a long, thin face, Gachet lived in a large
house with his two teenage children. Outside he kept dogs,
cats, rabbits, pigeons, ducks, a goat, a tortoise, and a
peacock. He advocated then-controversial concepts such
as socialism, cremation, and organ donation. His fond-
ness for the dead went to extremes: on the walls of his
attic he hung the death masks of criminals executed by
guillotine.

"I have seen Dr. Gachet," van Gogh wrote to Theo,
"who gives me the impression of being rather eccentric,
but his experience as a doctor must keep him balanced
enough to combat the nervous trouble from which he
certainly seems to be suffering at least as seriously as I."
Gachet's condition struck a kindred chord with van Gogh,
who soon wrote to his sister Wilhelmina that Gachet was
"a true friend . . . something like another brother." Van
Gogh dined regularly with the doctor, who promised his

*In Auvers, van Gogh tried
to capture the wide-open
landscape around the village,
such as in his* Landscape
with Carriage and Train in the
Background, *painted in June
1890. During the 70 days that
he lived in Auvers, van Gogh
painted some 70 canvases.*

new friend, Vincent told his sister, "that if the melancholy or anything else became too much for me to bear, he could easily do something to lessen its intensity. . . . Well, the moment when I need him may certainly come, however up to now all is well."

Van Gogh threw himself into his work in Auvers. He rose at dawn, drank little, and retired to bed early. In order to capture the wide-open landscape around the village, he took to using a double-square canvas—two square canvases side by side—which were ideal for panoramas. As usual, his productivity knew no bounds: for the nearly 70 days he lived in Auvers, he churned out on average one painting per day. Anton Hirschig, a Dutch painter who lived in the same inn as van Gogh, recalled that his compatriot placed each newly completed work "helter-skelter in the dirtiest little corner one can imagine, a sort of hovel where goats were usually kept. It was dark there, the walls were of brick without any plaster, with straw hanging from them. . . . And every day he brought new ones in; they were strewn on the floor and hanging on the walls. No one," he added, "ever looked at them."

But because he did not expect anyone to look at his pictures, van Gogh remained in good spirits—and more important, good health—well into June. On a Sunday, June 8, Theo and his family came for a visit. Vincent met them at the Auvers train station, bringing along a bird's nest as a plaything for his infant nephew. "He insisted upon carrying the baby and had no rest until he had shown him all the animals in [Gachet's] yard," Johanna wrote later. "We lunched in the open air, and afterward took a long walk, the day was so peacefully quiet, so happy."

As van Gogh knew all too well, such happiness could not last. The turning point came at the end of the month. On June 30, Theo wrote his brother a long letter bearing two bits of depressing news. First, after their picnic a fortnight before, little Vincent had fallen seriously ill. "You've never heard anything so grievously distressing as this almost continuous plaintive crying all through many days and many nights," Theo told him. But that the baby was now better did not ease the news that Theo then went on to relate: he had come to such loggerheads with his conservative employers at Goupil's that he was considering quitting his job and striking off on his own as an independent dealer. He admitted such a venture would be risky, but in the letter he tried to reassure his brother:

> Don't bother your head about me or about us, old fellow, but remember that what gives me the greatest pleasure is the knowledge that you are in good health and busy with your work, which is admirable. You already have too much fire, and we must be in a good shape to fight for a long time yet, for we shall have to battle all our lives rather than eat the oats of charity they give to old horses in the stables of the great. We shall draw the plow until our strength forsakes us, and we shall still look with admiration at the sun or the moon.

To the penniless Vincent, who had relied on his brother for his very existence—both as a painter and as a human being—for countless years, the news that his financial welfare was in danger came as a lethal blow. He immediately paid a visit to Theo in Paris, perhaps to try to talk him out of his plans. But he found no solace there. Theo and Johanna were exhausted from caring for their sleeplessly ill baby. After the warmth and joy the three had felt on his first visit to their house—not to mention their recent picnic—their seeming aloofness unsettled Vincent, as did visits from Toulouse-Lautrec and Aurier, the critic who had written the laudatory article about him. He left Paris feeling that, as he wrote Theo soon after their visit, "the prospect grows darker, I see no happy future at all."

Back in Auvers, he quarreled with his friend Gachet about a trivial matter, a painting by another painter that Gachet had not yet framed. "I think we must not count on Dr. Gachet *at all,*" he insisted to Theo. "First of all, he is sicker than I am. . . . Now when one blind man leads another, don't they both fall into the ditch?" Johanna tried to calm him down with a soothing letter, but it only gave

One of the last paintings van Gogh produced was Roots and Tree Trunks, *in which he adopted a darker palette and created an up close, abstract, and twisting view of nature. The painting seems to have been "framed and focused" like a photograph; he often used photographic reproductions of works by Delacroix and Millet as models, and he even sent photographs of his own artwork to his friends.*

van Gogh an excuse to explain in a follow-up letter how Theo's decision had shattered his sense of well-being:

> It is no slight thing when all of us feel our daily bread in danger; it is not a trifle when for other reasons also we feel that our existence is fragile. Back here, I still felt very sad and continued to feel the weight of the storm which threatens you. What can be done? You see, I generally try to be fairly cheerful, but my life too is menaced at its very root, and my steps also are wavering. I feared—not so much, but a little just the same—that being a burden to you, you felt me to be rather a thing to be dreaded.

He continued to paint, "though the brush almost slipped from my fingers." Two paintings executed in mid-July reveal the two alternating states of mind he seemed to have felt in the closing weeks of his life: absolute calm and utter despair. The first, *Wheat Fields Under Clouded Sky,* is serene. In what turned out to be his last letter to his mother and sister, van Gogh wrote that he was "quite absorbed in the immense plain with wheat fields against the hills, boundless as a sea, delicate yellow, delicate soft green, the delicate violet of a dug-up and weeded piece of soil, checkered at regular intervals under a sky of delicate blue, white, pink, violet tones. I am in a mood of almost too much calmness, in the mood to paint this."

His state of mind was as delicate as the colors he described, as the second painting reveals so tragically.

Crows over the Wheat Field, one of his last paintings, virtually shouts out the anguish he felt. The dark blue sky seems to crush down atop the wheat field, which pushes toward the viewer like a cresting wave. The brushstrokes are short, feverish stabs of paint; the crows are mere slashes of black. An ocher-lined path comes to an abrupt dead end in the middle of the painting. Indeed, to the viewer, as no doubt to Vincent, there seems to be no escape from this swirling, claustrophobic hell.

Referring to the work, Vincent wrote to Theo that he was putting the final touches on a painting of "vast fields of wheat under troubled skies, and I did not need to go out of my way to express sadness and extreme loneliness." David Sweetman, a van Gogh biographer, sees this painting as "the last cry of the haunted artist living out his anguish in paint. Here surely is Vincent, the angst-ridden father of the modern movement, of Fauvism, Expressionism, Abstract Expressionism, progenitor of any art in which the tortured personality of the artist is the paramount feature of the work."

On Sunday, July 27, van Gogh left the inn carrying his easel and a revolver he used to scare away the crows while he was working. He walked a few hundred yards from the inn, turned into a farmyard, and shot himself below the heart. Somehow he managed to stumble back to his room, where the innkeeper found him lying on his bed, his face to the wall. The innkeeper summoned Dr. Gachet, who examined van Gogh and pronounced that he might very well survive. "Then I will have to do it all over again," van Gogh said dolefully. Since he refused to give Gachet his brother's home address, the doctor sent an urgent message to Theo at his office. In the meantime, Gachet and the local Auvers doctor, Jean Mazery, decided not to try to remove the bullet. Safe surgical techniques had not yet been developed, and they felt removing it might worsen his condition.

Throughout the night, van Gogh lay in his bed wide awake, smoking a pipe and speaking not a word to anyone.

When Theo appeared at his bedside the next day, he implored him, "Do not cry, I did it for the good of everybody." The brothers continued to talk throughout the day, which gave Theo confidence enough to write to Johanna that evening, "Don't be too worried; once before things looked desperate for him and yet his strong nature eventually cheated the doctors." Yet in the same letter, Theo revealed a profound sadness about his older brother: "Poor fellow, fate has not given him much and he has no illusions left. Things are sometimes too hard, he feels so alone. . . . He inquired most urgently about you and the boy and said that he had not expected that life would bring him so many sorrows. If only we could give him a little courage to live!"

They could not. Around one o'clock on Tuesday morning, July 29, 1890, less than 36 hours after he had shot himself, van Gogh said weakly in Dutch, "I wish I could go home now," and died. He was 37 years old.

On August 1, in a letter to Aurier, Émile Bernard, a painter and close friend of van Gogh's, described the funeral, which was held in Auvers a few days later:

> On the walls of the room where his body lay all his last canvases were nailed, forming something like a halo around him and rendering—through the brilliance or genius which shone from them—his death even more deplorable for us artists. On the coffin a simple white drapery and masses of flowers, the sunflowers he loved so much, yellow dahlias, yellow flowers everywhere. It was his favorite color, if you remember, symbol of the light of which he dreamed in the hearts of men as well as in works of art. Near him also his easel, his folding stool and his brushes had been placed on the floor in front of the coffin. . . . At three o'clock the body was removed. His friends carried it to the hearse. Some of the people in the assembly wept. Theodorus van Gogh, who adored his brother, who had always sustained him in his struggle for art and independence, sobbed pitifully without cease. . . . Outside, the sun was ferociously hot. We climbed the hill of Auvers talking of him, of the bold forward thrust he has given to art, of the great projects that always preoccupied him, of

the good he has done to each of us. We arrived at the cemetery, a little new cemetery dotted with fresh tomb-stones. It is on a height overlooking the fields ready for reaping, under a wide blue sky he might still have loved—maybe. And then he was lowered into the grave. Who would not have cried at that moment—the day was too much to his liking to prevent us from thinking that he could still have lived happily.

On August 5, Theo wrote a letter to his sister Elisabeth telling her about the last conversation he had had with Vincent:

> [Vincent] himself wanted to die. When I . . . tried to convince him that we would cure him and that we hoped he would be spared further attacks, he replied: 'There is no end to sorrow.' I thought then that I understood what he meant. He was very calm. Soon afterwards he was shaken by a fresh spasm and, a minute later, closed his eyes.

On the day Vincent died, Theo discovered an unfinished letter his brother had addressed to him in which he discussed his work: "Since the thing that matters most is going well, why should I say more about things of less importance? . . . before we have a chance to talk business more collectedly. . . . Well, my own work, I am risking my life for it and my reason has half foundered because of it—. . . . but *que veux-tu* [what do you want]?"

Theo was undone by Vincent's death. Losing Vincent was like losing a part of himself. He returned to Paris a man emotionally broken. "One cannot write how grieved one is nor find any solace," he wrote to his mother. "It is a grief that will last and which I shall never forget as long as I live; the only thing one might say is that he himself had found the rest he so much longed for. . . . Life was such a burden to him; but now, as often happens, everybody is full of praise for his talents. . . . Oh, Mother! He was so my own, own brother."

Over the coming months, Theo set a single goal for himself: to preserve Vincent's memory and art. He traveled to Holland to have his family sign over Vincent's estate to him, in order to better conserve it. He approached the critic G.-Albert Aurier about writing a biography of his brother. A van Gogh fan to the last, Aurier willingly agreed and promised to tackle it as soon as he finished a novel he was working on. But he never got the chance, for two years later, at age 27, he died of typhoid fever. Theo also asked the well-known art dealer Paul Durand-Ruel if he would set up an exhibition of his brother's paintings. Durand-Ruel had lost money staging shows of works by Monet, Renoir, and others, and so refused. Theo tried to rent Le Tambourin, the café where five years before Vincent had organized his own show of Japanese prints—also to no avail. Undaunted, he fell back on the idea of installing a show in his own apartment.

But fate would have none of it. Grief had taken a greater toll on Theo than anyone could have imagined, and by now he was, by his own admission, cadaverously thin. Tragically, his mental state proved even more fragile. In a letter to his son Lucien, Camille Pissarro described Theo's sudden and wholly unexpected slip into madness:

> It appears that Theo van Gogh was ill before his madness; he had uremia. For a week he was unable to urinate; added to that were the worries, the sadness, and a violent argument with his employers concerning a Decamps painting. [Alexandre-Gabriel Decamps won a Grand Medal for his paintings in the Salon of 1855, and was primarily known as an Orientalist, depicting Turkish and Arabian subjects.] As a result of all this, in a moment of exasperation, he thanked the Boussods [his employers] and suddenly went mad. He wanted to rent Le Tambourin in order to form an association of artists. Finally he became violent. He, who so loved his wife and child, wanted to kill them. In brief, they had to put him in Dr. [Emile] Blanche's sanatorium.

Although Theo had never before shown any signs of mental instability, it sadly ran in his family. Besides Vincent, there was Wilhelmina, their youngest sister, who, within a few years of Vincent's death, went mad herself. She was committed to an asylum, where, after speaking hardly a word for nearly half a century, she died in 1941 at the age of 79.

At first, Theo's illness seemed more tragic than seriously incapacitating. Like Vincent with his erstwhile obsession with obscure biblical quotations, Theo mailed bizarre missives to his friends. He sent a telegram to Gauguin in Brittany: "Departure to tropics assured, money follows—Theo, Director." (Theo had no money to send and he was director of nothing.) When Theo seemed to have recovered well enough to travel, Johanna, feeling a change of scene would do him good, took him and little Vincent to Utrecht, Holland, where she had taught school before marrying.

But Theo fell into a profound depression. The career and comfortable life that he had so carefully built up over the years had disintegrated, and he had lost his best friend in the world—indeed, one could say his reason for being. To get him treatment, Johanna admitted him to an asylum in Utrecht. There, in midwinter, he suffered from a stroke. He died on January 25, 1891, at age 33. Little Vincent was not even a year old, and his uncle Vincent dead not six months. Theo's physician wrote simply that he had died from "overstrain and sorrow; he had a life full of emotional stress." Johanna buried him in Holland, but more than two decades later, in 1914, she had his remains reburied next to Vincent's in the Auvers cemetery. There, as a memorial, she planted a sprig of ivy from Gachet's garden. In the years since, the ivy has spread across both graves, uniting the two in one broad, green bed.

To assuage her own grief, Johanna began reading the great stack of Vincent's letters that Theo had carefully saved, in order to find any mention of her husband. Soon after Theo's funeral, Johanna returned to Paris, where she confided to a friend: "The first evening that I spent again in our home, I turned to the bundle of letters because I knew I would meet him in them, and night after night I found solace there from my great misery. In those days I was not looking for Vincent but only for Theo, for every detail that concerned him. . . ." She had been married to Theo for only 18 months—and the days she had spent with Vincent amounted to less than a week.

Soon, however, she became as obsessed as Vincent was with his work—or Theo was with Vincent—in a drive to secure the posterity of her brother-in-law. Not surprisingly, she went at it alone. Even her brother, the painter Andries Bonger, who had been a friend of Vincent's, advised her to get rid of the huge mass of work van Gogh left behind, which included several hundred drawings and 550 paintings. But she persevered. Like her husband before her, she immediately got the van Gogh family to sign over Theo's estate—and thus, Vincent's—to her son, little Vincent. Then she set off on what became a decades-long mission to assure van Gogh's proper place in the history of the modern art movement.

Van Gogh's fame rose slowly. In 1892, Émile Bernard put on a small memorial show in Paris that included 16 paintings. Nine years passed before the next show, a retrospective of van Gogh's work, appeared in the Galerie Bernheim-Jeune in Paris in 1901. In 1905, Amsterdam's Stedelijk Museum put on a major exhibition organized by Johanna and her new husband, John Cohen Gosschalk, whom she had married in 1901. During this time, a Berlin art dealer named Paul Cassirer, a great fan of van Gogh's, also began to spread the word about the Dutch painter—and sell his paintings—in Germany.

Through Johanna's efforts, van Gogh's reputation continued to grow. In 1912, two major exhibitions brought van Gogh to a wider European audience: a Postimpressionist exhibition in London that included 21 of his paintings, and a modern art exhibition in Cologne, Germany, that featured 108 of his paintings. Two years later, Johanna reached another goal she had set for herself: she arranged to have a three-volume edition of Vincent's letters published in Amsterdam. Featuring each letter in its original language, the book also bore a lengthy introduction by Johanna. By 1929, when the Museum of Modern Art in New York put on a major retrospective showcasing the work of the four artists seen to be the major movers and shakers of the modern art movement—Cézanne, Gauguin, Seurat, and van Gogh—Johanna's mission had been accomplished.

Her son, Vincent, who became an engineer, went on to donate his van Gogh collection—the largest ever assembled—to the Rijksmuseum, Holland's major art museum. The Rijksmuseum responded in kind. In 1973, it inaugurated the Rijksmuseum Vincent van Gogh, an entire museum devoted to one of the country's foremost painters. Today, van Gogh is one of the best loved of modern artists. Indeed, the picture of the yellow chair he used in Arles is the most widely reproduced work of nonreligious art. And the artist who sold but one painting during his lifetime would probably be shocked to learn that one of his works, the *Portrait of Dr. Gachet* (June 1890), was sold on May 15, 1990, at Christie's auction house in New York for $82.5 million, the highest price ever paid for a single painting to date.

In his short, intense life, this erstwhile preacher, so filled with emotion yet so tortured by his inability to connect with others, succeeded in creating a timeless, highly personal art that profoundly touches people. In a letter to Theo in 1883, when he was first taking up his brush, van Gogh humbly summed up his mission as an artist: "The world concerns me only insofar as I feel a certain indebtedness and duty toward it because I have walked this earth for 30 years, and, out of gratitude, want to leave some souvenir in the shape of drawings or pictures—not made to please a certain taste in art, but to express a sincere human feeling." Van Gogh's millions of admirers around the world attest to how well he succeeded.

FURTHER READING

Auden, W. H., ed. *Van Gogh: A Self-Portrait*. Greenwich, CT: New York Graphic Society, 1961.

The Complete Letters of Vincent Van Gogh. Vols. I–III. New York: New York Graphic Society, 1978.

Cooper, Douglas. *Van Gogh Drawings and Watercolors*. New York: Macmillan, 1955.

Leymarie, Jean. *Van Gogh*. New York: Portland House, 1987.

Pickvance, Ronald. *Van Gogh in Saint-Rémy and Auvers*. New York: The Metropolitan Museum of Art, 1986.

Schapiro, Meyer. *Vincent van Gogh*. The Library of Great Painters. New York: Harry N. Abrams, 1950.

Stone, Irving, ed. *Dear Theo: The Autobiography of Vincent van Gogh*. Garden City, NY: Doubleday, 1946.

Sweetman, David. *Van Gogh: His Life and His Art*. New York: Crown, 1990.

Van der Wolk, Johannes, et al. *Vincent van Gogh: Drawings*. New York: Rizzoli, 1990.

Van Uitert, Evert, et al. *Vincent van Gogh: Paintings*. New York: Rizzoli, 1990.

Wallace, Robert. *The World of Van Gogh*. New York: Time-Life Books, 1969.

Zurcher, Bernard. *Vincent Van Gogh: Art, Life, and Letters*. San Diego, CA: Thunder Bay Press, 1985.

CHRONOLOGY

1851	Reverend Theodorus van Gogh and Anna Cornelius Carbentus are married in Groot Zundert, a village in Holland's Brabant region
1852	The "first Vincent," Vincent Willem van Gogh, is stillborn on March 30
1853	Vincent Willem van Gogh, the "second Vincent," is born on March 30 in Zundert
1857	Vincent's brother Theodorus, called Theo, is born on May 1
1866	Vincent enters school at Tilburg
1868	Vincent suddenly leaves school and returns to Zundert
1869	Vincent is hired by art dealers Goupil and Company to work at their gallery in The Hague
1870	Van Gogh meets artist Anton Mauve, who becomes his cousin by marriage
1872	Vincent begins his lifelong correspondence with his brother Theo
1873	Theo joins Goupil's Brussels branch in January; Vincent moves to the London office of Goupil's in May; Vincent boards with the Loyers and falls in love with Eugénie Loyer but he is spurned by her; Theo is transferred to the Goupil's office in The Hague
1874	Vincent is sent to Goupil's Paris office in October and stays until December, when he goes back to London
1875	Returns to the Paris office of Goupil's, but he loses interest in work and studies the Bible and visits museums instead; van Gogh visits his parents in Etten during Christmas
1876	Vincent resigns from Goupil's in April and goes to Ramsgate, near London, to work as a teacher; in July he becomes an assistant at Isleworth and preaches to the poor
1878	Enrolls in school for lay preachers in Brussels, Belgium, in August; starts missionary work in December in the Borinage, a poor coal-mining region of Belgium
1879	He devotes himself to helping the miners in the Borinage, but his fervor is deemed excessive by his superiors and they dismiss him; he lives among the miners and increasingly applies himself to drawing
1880	Decides to become an artist, with encouragement and financial support from Theo, and begins drawing studies at the Brussels Academy in October
1881	Moves to Etten in April; he falls in love with his first cousin Kee Vos, who rejects him
1882	Painter Anton Mauve teaches him oil painting in The Hague; begins his relationship with Christien Clasina Maria Hoornik, called Sien; Vincent's parents settle in Nuenen
1883	Leaves Sien, and moves to Drenthe, a peat-bog region in northern Holland, in September to paint peasant life; van Gogh lives with his parents in Nuenen in December

1884   Margot Begemann, a neighbor, falls in love with Vincent, who rejects her advances; she tries to commit suicide; in his paintings, he portrays weavers and peasants at work

1885   Reverend Theodorus van Gogh dies on March 26; Vincent executes his painting *The Potato Eaters;* moves to Antwerp in November

1886   Van Gogh enrolls in art classes at the Antwerp Academy in January; joins his brother Theo, a successful art dealer, in Paris in March; studies with Fernand Cormon in Montmartre and meets Émile Bernard, Henri de Toulouse-Lautrec, Camille Pissarro, Paul Signac, and Paul Gauguin

1887   Vincent exhibits paintings at Le Tambourin café

1888   Moves to Arles in southern France in February to establish an "artists colony"; painter Paul Gauguin arrives in Arles in October; Theo announces his engagement to Johanna Bonger early in December; on December 23 van Gogh has a nervous breakdown, cuts off part of his ear, and is admitted to the Arles hospital under the care of Dr. Rey

1889   Theo and Johanna are married on April 17; on May 8, Vincent voluntarily admits himself to the asylum in Saint-Rémy-de-Provence, near Arles, run by Dr. Peyron; paints *The Starry Night* in June; on December 23, he eats paints and guzzles kerosene in a suicide attempt

1890   In January, *The Red Vineyards,* the only painting to be sold in van Gogh's lifetime, is bought by Anna Boch at a Les Vingt exhibition, and the only article written about him during his lifetime is published; the "third Vincent," van Gogh's nephew, is born on January 31; van Gogh has an attack on February 22; on May 16, he leaves Saint-Rémy and visits Theo and his family in Paris; moves to Auvers-sur-Oise, near Paris, in May and is under the care of Dr. Gachet; Theo and his family visit Vincent in Auvers in mid-June; Vincent shoots himself below the heart on July 27 and dies in Theo's arms two days later at the age of 37; he is buried in Auvers on July 30; Theo goes mad in October; Johanna takes Theo back to Holland

1891   Theo dies in Utrecht, Holland, of chronic nephritis (acute inflammation of the kidney) on January 25, at age 33

1901   The first retrospective of van Gogh's artwork (71 works) is exhibited in Paris

1907   Anna van Gogh, Vincent's mother, dies at the age of 88

1914   Johanna has Theo's body reburied next to Vincent's

1990   *Portrait of Dr. Gachet* is sold for $82.5 million at auction, the highest amount ever paid for a painting at the time

INDEX

PICTURE CREDITS

Alinari/Art Resource, NY: p. 76; Art Resource, NY: pp. 19, 54, 65, 105, 108, 115; Bridgman Art Library/Art Resource, NY: p. 26; Foto Marburg/Art Resource, NY: pp. 2, 23, 60, 73, 97; Gemeente-museum, The Hague: p. 37; Giraudon/Art Resource, NY: pp. 12, 14, 41, 68, 77, 82, 89, 90; Erich Lessing/Art Resource: pp. 66, 67, 69, 98; The Museum of Modern Art, NY: p. 72; Rijksmuseum Kröller-Müller, Otterlo: pp. 44, 49, 78; Scala/Art Resource, NY: pp. 111, 112; Rudolf Staechelin Foundation, on extended loan to the Oeffentliche Kunstsammlung Basel: pp. 70–71; Vincent van Gogh Foundation/van Gogh Museum, Amsterdam: cover, pp. 28, 30, 34, 52, 85, 110.

Peter Tyson minored in art history at Trinity College in Hartford, Connecticut. A science writer and editor for 12 years, he began his career at *Omni* magazine in New York in 1983 and is currently managing editor of *Earthwatch* magazine in Watertown, Massachusetts. An inveterate traveler, he has visited many remote regions, including Antarctica, Madagascar, Tibet, and Siberia. Mr. Tyson resides in Arlington, Massachusetts, with his wife and two children.

Jerry Lewis is the National Chairman of the Muscular Dystrophy Association (MDA) and host of the MDA Labor Day Telethon. An internationally acclaimed comedian, Lewis began his entertainment career in New York and then performed in a comedy team with singer and actor Dean Martin from 1946 to 1956. Lewis has appeared in many films—including *The Delicate Delinquent, Rock a Bye Baby, The Bellboy, Cinderfella, The Nutty Professor, The Disorderly Orderly,* and *The King of Comedy*—and his comedy performances, such as his 1995 role in the Broadway play *Damn Yankees,* continue to delight audiences around the world.

John Callahan is a nationally syndicated cartoonist and the author of an illustrated autobiography, *Don't Worry, He Won't Get Far on Foot.* He has also produced three cartoon collections: *Do Not Disturb Any Further, Digesting the Child Within,* and *Do What He Says! He's Crazy!!!* He has recently been the subject of feature articles in the *New York Times Magazine,* the *Los Angeles Times Magazine,* and the *Cleveland Plain Dealer,* and has been profiled on "60 Minutes." Callahan resides in Portland, Oregon.